IKE / Abilene to Berlin

IKE / Abilene to Berlin

The life of Dwight D. Eisenhower from his childhood in Abilene, Kansas, through his command of
the Allied forces in Europe in World War II

by Stephen E. Ambrose

Illustrated with maps and photographs

Harper & Row, Publishers
New York, Evanston, San Francisco, London

IKE: Abilene to Berlin
Copyright © 1973 by Stephen E. Ambrose

LIBRARY OF CONGRESS CATALOG CARD NUMBER: 73–5474
TRADE STANDARD BOOK NUMBER: 06–020075–8
HARPERCREST STANDARD BOOK NUMBER: 06–020076–6

FIRST EDITION

For Barry

contents

Meeting Eisenhower / ix

chapter one / **Command Decision** / 1

chapter two / **Abilene, Sweet Abilene** / 10

chapter three / **West Point** / 29

chapter four / **A Period of Preparation (1915–1929)** / 41

chapter five / **The Long and Dreary Thirties** / 62

chapter six / **Marshall Grooms Ike for High Command** / 80

chapter seven / **Lighting the TORCH** / 98

chapter eight / **The Battle for Kasserine Pass** / 115

chapter nine / **Sicily and Italy** / 125

chapter ten / **Preparing OVERLORD** / 139

chapter eleven / **The Trouble with Monty** / 153

chapter twelve / **The Battle of the Bulge** / 171

chapter thirteen / **The Last Decision: Berlin** / 186

further reading / 207

glossary / 210

acknowledgments / 213

index / 215

about the author / 221

Meeting Eisenhower

I'm an extremely lucky historian, for I was privileged to be able to interview the man whose career I spent six years studying. I first met Dwight Eisenhower during the winter of 1965, when he was living on his Pennsylvania farm. His office was near the farm, on the edge of the lovely campus of Gettysburg College. Ike and his small staff took up an entire house. Although he was retired, no former United States President can really escape work, and Eisenhower ordinarily spent six or more hours a day in his office. He would answer his mail, consult with politicians, grant interviews to historians, and dictate his presidential memoirs.

My purpose in seeing Eisenhower was to go over his personal papers with him, a rare opportunity for any historian. Before this time, Presidents' personal papers had only been published long after their deaths, which meant that the scholars who edited their papers and prepared them for publication could not clear up difficult points with the Presidents themselves. Ike, however, believed that the public had a right to know what he had done during his career, why he had made certain decisions, and what his views were on every problem he had dealt with. He therefore decided to publish his personal letters, orders, telegrams, memoranda, and, indeed, anything he had ever written, as soon as a team of independent scholars had prepared them in book form. He gave the publishing rights to The Johns Hopkins University, of which his brother Dr. Milton Eisenhower was President, and the University chose Dr. Alfred D. Chandler, Jr., as editor. I was chosen as associate editor. In his deed of gift, Ike expressly stated that there would be no censorship, by either himself or his family, of what we published.

Our job, essentially, was to select documents for publication, then write footnotes that would identify people, places, and events, and explain complex subjects that Ike had only touched upon. Often enough Ike would mention a person or an event we could not identify. In other instances we would be unable to understand Ike's position on, or view of, a particular issue. Dr. Chandler and I had been hard at work for well over a year when we made our first trip to Gettysburg, and we certainly had a lot of questions.

I was scared. It is not, after all, an everyday occurrence for a twenty-nine-year-old junior professor to meet, much less question, an American President and five-star general. But I was fascinated by Ike's career and eager to ask questions. So I plunged ahead—or rather stayed right behind Dr. Chandler.

One of Eisenhower's aides, a two-star general, showed us into his office. It was simply furnished and comfortable. There were two original paintings of rural scenes by Andrew Wyeth on the walls, a handsome row of bookcases, and a scattering of leather-covered chairs.

Ike sat behind his large desk, with a few papers and a couple of books in front of him. He glanced at us, grinned, stood up, spread his arms, grinned some more, and shook hands. It was a remarkable experience: Ike had a unique ability to establish a mood in a room. Without making any evident effort, he dominated. But it was not a heavy-handed domination, for he immediately focused on his visitors' concerns and got onto their wavelength. He directed his own attention, and that of everyone in the room, to the discussion at hand. Most of all, he put us at ease. The atmosphere he created was so relaxed that I forgot to be awed, impressed, and afraid, and began to ask questions.

Within half an hour, Ike had his tie pulled down, his suit coat slung over the back of his chair, his shirt-sleeves rolled up, and was graphically explaining what his fears and worries had been in 1942 during the Battle for Kasserine Pass. His exclamation points were solid four-letter words, spoken without any embarrassment. After all, he had been a professional soldier for more than three decades, and his language was a reflection of that career. He spoke quickly, in complete sentences, indeed in polished paragraphs.

He was enjoying himself enormously, refighting the North African campaign of World War II, commenting on Nazi Field Marshal Erwin Rommel's strengths and weaknesses, recalling his discovery of Omar Bradley's capabilities, remembering his first meeting with British General Bernard Montgomery, and so on. But then his secretary informed us that the editors of Ike's presidential memoirs* had arrived and had been waiting a good long while. It was time for us to go.

When the editors of the presidential memoirs came in, the damndest thing happened. Right in front of our eyes, in a matter of seconds, Ike rolled down his sleeves, pulled up his tie, put on his coat, sat up straight, and changed from being a two-star general in the mud of North Africa to being the President of the United States. Now he spoke slowly, considering every word. The enthusiasm was gone from his voice; his sentences dangled; he wandered from topic to topic. Most noticeable of all, there were no more four-letter words.

In my many subsequent interviews with Eisenhower I learned that while he had a sharp memory, he was not much interested in politics. The selectivity of his memory,

---

* Ike's presidential memoirs were later published in two volumes, called *The White House Years: A Personal Account*. He had already written his World War II memoirs, *Crusade in Europe*, one of the best-selling books of this century. There are two major differences between his war memoirs and the work Dr. Chandler and I were editing, *The Papers of Dwight D. Eisenhower: The War Years*. First, the *Papers* are much more complete. For example, in the *Papers* it took five volumes of nearly 800 pages each to cover Ike's war career; in his war memoirs, Ike covered the same period in 400 pages. The second difference is that in his memoirs Ike tells what he *remembered* about the war, while in the *Papers* we can read what he actually wrote at the time.

in fact, was a good key to his feelings. He remembered relatively little about the political issues of World War II, or even about his own actions when they had been political. But he could recall the name of every one of his division commanders, tell us something about the personality of each, give the division's location at any specific time during the campaigns in Europe, and even remember which German units had been opposing it. When we discussed something he had done as a soldier he would make detailed and highly quotable comments, but when we discussed politics he would usually shake his head and dismiss the subject. He had been a soldier for thirty-five years, a politician for only eight years, and it was obvious that he enjoyed soldiering more than politics.

Ike was unusual in many ways. For example, he had decided on early publication of his papers not because he was worried about his historical reputation, or to justify his actions and prove that he was right, but in order to help historians and the public in general understand the problems he had dealt with. The Sioux Indians have a saying: "Never criticize a man until you have walked a mile in his moccasins." Ike hoped that after reading his papers and recognizing the scope and magnitude of the decisions he had made both as a general and as President, people would make kinder, or at least more understanding, judgments.

Two related controversies about his generalship during the war always set Ike off on long discourses. His hands would flash through the air, his facial expression would change with each sentence—and he did have a marvelously expressive face. The first charge (made primarily by British General Bernard Montgomery) was that Ike had been an excessively cautious general, afraid to take risks, and as a result the war had dragged on much longer than it should have. The second charge was that Ike had practically given the city of Berlin to the Red Army, when he could have taken it with British or American troops and held it for the western Allies.

Eisenhower thought of himself as a great risk-taker. He would lean forward, fix his eyes on mine, and with great seriousness tick off the military operations he had ordered and carried out successfully, though both his superiors and subordinates had insisted that such operations were much too risky. On the question of capturing Berlin before the Russians, he maintained that it would have been impossible militarily, and would have made no political difference anyway, because the occupation boundaries for postwar Germany had already been set by Churchill, Roosevelt, and Stalin in their Yalta meeting.

He was certainly right about the importance of studying his papers before judging the role he had played. The criticism he resented most was that he had been merely a "chairman of the board," a nice guy with a big grin and nothing more. According to some of his critics, Ike —both as a soldier and as a politician—had been the man at the top who saw to it that everybody got along, but left the decision-making process to his underlings. When I began work on the papers, I'd been one of those who thought of him as "chairman of the board." But after a year of intensive study I completely changed my mind and became one of his great admirers—so much so that anything I write about him is partisan. I'm not alone. When The Johns Hopkins Press published the first five volumes of Eisenhower's papers, *The War Years*, in 1970, they were hailed by reviewers in scholarly journals, popular magazines, and newspapers. Nearly every reviewer said that his opinion of Eisenhower had been changed by this information. Seeing the problems of World War II from Ike's point of view made people realize what a decisive general he had been and how invaluable he was to the final victory. Since the publication of *The War Years*, Eisenhower's reputation as a soldier has risen steadily. His presidential papers, now being edited, will soon be published. When they are, it is likely that his reputation as a politician will also go up.

Ike was the kindest, most thoughtful human being I have ever known. You couldn't help but like him. Not only was he totally honest, quite willing to admit and discuss mistakes he had made without trying to hide anything, but he was also truly concerned about how other people were getting along. During one critical stage of the war, when he had to make some tough decisions, he discovered that a plane was leaving London for Cairo, Egypt, with an empty seat. He knew that his secretary was engaged to marry a young man stationed in Cairo, so he took time to arrange a leave for her so she could fly to Egypt to see her future husband. As one other small example, he always worried about where Dr. Chandler and I could find a good meal on our way home from Gettysburg to Baltimore. He had made the drive many times and swore there was not a single decent restaurant on the road. He used to warn us against particular restaurants.

In my last interview with Eisenhower, a few months

before his death, I asked him what his greatest disappointment had been. He replied instantly: "The failure to achieve peace." He faulted himself as President for not having created the conditions that would have brought about a real and permanent peace. Given the nature of the Cold War, however, and the differing aims of the United States and the Soviet Union during that period, peace had never been a real possibility—at least not the kind of permanent peace Eisenhower was talking about. What he did achieve was a breathing spell in the Cold War; and not incidentally, he saved the lives of thousands of young American men who might otherwise have been fighting in Southeast Asia ten years earlier.

In my view, Eisenhower was one of the great generals of World War II, and one of the best America ever produced. This view is substantiated, I believe, by *The War Years*. No considered judgment of Eisenhower's presidency can be made until his presidential papers have been published. His most important accomplishment, nevertheless, is clear. For eight years he kept the peace. Eight years of peace, in the highly charged atmosphere of the Cold War, was Eisenhower's finest achievement. In the end, this great soldier, the conqueror of the mighty German Army, was a man of peace.

IKE / Abilene to Berlin

chapter one
Command Decision

General Dwight Eisenhower awoke. It was 4 A.M., June 5, 1944. Tomorrow, if all went well, the invasion of Nazi-occupied Europe would begin.

Ike shook the sleep from his head, pulled himself out of bed, and opened the door of his trailer. The rain was coming down in almost horizontal streaks, the wind roaring. Muttering gloomily to himself, he turned back and began to dress. After putting on his officer's jacket with the four stars on the shoulders, he slipped on his raincoat, tugged his hat down tightly on his nearly bald head, and went out to a waiting jeep. He barely grumbled a reply to the driver's cheery "Good morning!" and set out for his headquarters at Southwick House, Portsmouth, in southeastern England, about a mile away.

As the jeep sloshed through the mud and rain Eisenhower, who had the lofty title of Supreme Commander, Allied Expeditionary Force, thought about his problems and responsibilities. Everything that the American, British, and Canadian forces—the Allies—had done during the previous three years of World War II had been directed toward this moment. If all went well, Allied troops would dash onto the beaches of Normandy, on the west coast of France, at dawn on D-Day—June 6, 1944. Eisenhower was confident that if his troops could get ashore, then capture and hold the Normandy area, he would be able to defeat the Germans. The Russian Red Army was driving the Germans back toward Berlin on the eastern front. If the Allies could attack from the west, using their superiority in tanks and guns, the Germans would be finished. But the Allies could not attack if they could not get ashore.

The invasion carried the code name OVERLORD, designed to confuse any German spies who might learn of it. Operation OVERLORD was the most thoroughly planned military undertaking in the history of mankind and the largest single action in the history of warfare. Hundreds of thousands of men were involved, along with six thousand ships and innumerable aircraft of all types. Eisenhower commanded the entire force—air and naval units as well as the ground troops. For the preceding five months he had worked day and night to prepare for all possible emergencies, for he knew that if OVERLORD failed, the Allies could possibly lose the war to Germany.

Eisenhower had prepared for everything, except the weather. On the morning of June 5, glancing out from his jeep, he shook his head again. The weather might ruin it all. A great storm had come in off the Atlantic Ocean and had hit the French coast. The waves were high and the wind was whipping them higher. The landing craft that would carry the infantry and tanks to shore were flat-bottomed, cumbersome vessels, and difficult to steer properly in a heavy sea. If Eisenhower ordered the invasion to go ahead despite the storm, the landing craft might flounder, drowning the men. There were other good reasons for delaying the invasion. The bad weather made it impossible for the Allied Air Force to bomb the German positions in Normandy and would also make the planned paratrooper airdrop behind German lines difficult at best.

But if there were factors that called for a decision to postpone the invasion, Ike thought, there were also strong arguments for starting immediately. In the first place, his weatherman had told him that there might be a break in the weather within twenty-four hours, bringing mild winds and calm seas to the Normandy beach at about dawn on June 6. That would be ideal—but of course it was only a prediction. Meanwhile, all Eisenhower could see around him was rain. All he could hear above the jeep's engine was the roar of the wind. Eisenhower decided he would wait and see what the weatherman had to say at the last meeting at Southwick House, where he was going now and where he would have to make the final decision.

If the weather news was favorable, Eisenhower was anxious to start. For five months he and his subordinates, all the generals and admirals serving under him who commanded the individual units of the invading force, had prepared for this day. The officers and men of the Allied Expeditionary Force wanted to get on with the job; any delay would make the already severe tension

Preparing for D-Day (above left), *landing craft are combat loaded in southern England. On D-Day minus one, Ike spends as much time as possible with his men, including American paratroopers who will drop behind enemy lines in a few hours.*

unbearable. A delay would also mean that they would have to wait another month, because the moon and tidal conditions would not again be suitable for an invasion until then. Surely there was at least one German spy in the vast army that had now been told that Normandy was the objective. Surely, if there was a delay, he would manage to get word to Hitler's high command that the Allies were coming to Normandy.

If Adolf Hitler, head of the German Nazi Party, knew where the invasion was going to hit, he could concentrate his defensive efforts there and build up a force so strong that no invading army, no matter how large, could defeat it. Eisenhower and his staff would have to plan an invasion for some other part of the French coast, a process that would take months. By then it would be winter, too late to invade Europe in 1944.

Delay or postponement of OVERLORD was a bad choice at best, but an unsuccessful invasion would be worse. Eisenhower, the only man who could decide, carried a heavy burden as he climbed out of his jeep and dashed through the rain into Southwick House.

Inside, in the mess room which served as a meeting place, hot coffee helped shake the gray mood and unsteady feeling. Eisenhower's chief staff officers and subordinate commanders were already there. The vast fleet that would carry the troops across the English Channel and provide gunfire support for the invasion was ready, its officers waiting only for Eisenhower's final word before starting.

The weatherman came in and repeated his prediction that the storm would lift and that conditions would be good on D-Day. Eisenhower thanked him and turned to his subordinates, led by Air Marshal Arthur Tedder, General Omar Bradley, and General Bernard Montgomery. He wanted to know what each one thought. Most wanted to start, but they all pointed out the problems that bad weather would create—the troops would arrive ashore, if they made it at all, seasick and unable to fight; the paratroopers would not be able to locate their drop zones and would end up scattered all through Normandy; the Navy's battleships would need luck to hit their targets if the sea was rolling; the Air Force would not be able to provide air cover for the invasion. If the weatherman's prediction was correct, then all should go well, but he could not guarantee, only predict. The ships were waiting—if there was to be an invasion on June 6 they had to get started now.

The Supreme Commander was the only man who could give the order. His Chief of Staff, General Walter Bedell Smith, was struck by the "loneliness and isolation of a commander at a time when such a momentous decision was to be taken by him, with full knowledge that failure or success rests on his individual decision."

Eisenhower thought for a moment, glanced around the room, then said quietly but clearly, "OK, let's go."

The commanders rushed from their chairs and dashed out to their command posts. Within thirty seconds the mess room was empty, except for Eisenhower. A minute earlier he had been the most powerful man in the world. Upon his word depended the fate of millions of men, not to mention great nations. The moment he uttered the word to go, however, he was powerless. For the next two or three days there was almost nothing he could do that would in any way change anything. The invasion could not be stopped—not by him, not by anyone except the German defenders or, more likely, the weather. Once started, the gigantic force had a momentum of its own. Eisenhower could only sit and wait, pray and hope.

Eisenhower spent the day visiting paratroopers who were preparing to climb aboard huge transport planes, to be dropped that night on the Normandy coast. The rain slowed, then stopped; the wind began to subside. His mood improved with the weather. Once he even saw a flash of sunshine and grinned broadly. Stopping for coffee, he played a game of checkers with an aide, the board on top of a cracker box. The aide was winning, two kings to one, when Eisenhower jumped one of the aide's kings and got a draw.

After dinner he visited with paratroopers from the U.S. 101st Airborne Division, which was just preparing to take off for France. As the last plane roared into the sky Eisenhower turned to his driver, his shoulders sagging visibly. A reporter thought he saw tears in the Supreme Commander's eyes—Eisenhower knew that the 101st would take heavy casualties and many of the men to whom he had just talked would be dead before morning. Eisenhower began to walk slowly toward his car. "Well," he said quietly, "it's on."

The drive back to his trailer took nearly two hours. Eisenhower arrived at 1:15 A.M., June 6. He sat around and chatted with some aides for a while, then finally went to bed. Shortly before 7 A.M. British Admiral Bertram Ramsay, who commanded the naval units, called to tell him everything was going according to plan. Then an aide came over to his trailer with good news—the air-drop had worked and the troops were going ashore in a calm sea. Over 156,000 American, British, and Canadian troops had breached Hitler's supposedly impregnable Atlantic Wall. Nazi control of Europe was doomed. The aide found the Supreme Commander of the entire expedition sitting up in bed, smoking a cigarette, and reading a Western novel.

chapter two

Abilene, Sweet Abilene

Who was this man who could make such great decisions with such confidence, and where did he come from?

Abilene was the town. Sweet Abilene. "Prettiest town I ever seen," according to the old-time cowboys. Abilene, Kansas, sits on the eastern edge of the Great Plains of North America, almost exactly in the geographical center of the United States. From 1867 to 1872 it was the capital of the Wild West, famous for its bars, its gunfighters, its tough U.S. Marshals (including "Wild Bill" Hickok), and most of all, its cattle. The cattle were there because the Kansas Pacific Railroad had laid tracks from Kansas City as far west as Abilene. Cowboys from Texas drove their herds along the trails northward to Abilene, the nearest railroad center, where the cattle were loaded onto cars and carried east to feed the big cities. By the time the cowboys arrived in Abilene they were hot, dusty, dirty, and thirsty. They had not seen a woman or had a drink in months. At "Hell's Half-Acre" just north of town, saloons, gambling halls, and bawdy houses met their needs.

Then the railroad laid tracks farther west and the cowboys no longer came to Abilene. It changed its character overnight, becoming a quiet little rural town with nothing to distinguish it from thousands of similar communities scattered throughout the country. Abilene's businessmen made their living by selling supplies to farmers in the area. Abilene's youngsters spent their working time on farms, in gardens, or at the local milk-processing plant, and their free time hunting, fishing, exploring, or playing baseball and football. Nothing much ever happened, but if it was dull it was also peaceful and friendly. Everyone knew everyone else in town and none of the homes had a lock on the door.

Abilene was pure America. In the summer it was as hot as New Orleans, in the winter as cold as Minneapolis. Spring days reminded settlers from New England of a late May afternoon in Vermont, while Indian summer brought back to transplanted Virginians memories of the glories of fall in the Blue Ridge Mountains. The wind always blew, bringing hot air from the Gulf of Mexico or cold blasts from the Rockies or from Canada, and sometimes even a little rain from the west. People lived in close contact with nature; the rhythm of life was set by the changing seasons.

After the cowboys moved on west Abilene was a commonplace little town, with all the strengths and weaknesses of an older, rural America. Abilene's citizens were remarkable only because they were so typical.

Yet Abilene did have one truly outstanding family—a family that was able to build on the enduring values of the past while ignoring, or overcoming at least, some of the pettiness, prejudice, and ignorance that was also a part of nineteenth-century rural America. And from that family came the man who would command America's largest army in the nation's largest war, then become President of the United States and deal with problems undreamed of in his Abilene boyhood. Both as a soldier and as a politician he would apply principles and values he learned as a boy in Abilene. Usually these would be enough to get the job done, frequently in spectacular fashion; sometimes they were, at best, simple and limited solutions to complex problems. But whether satisfactory or not, Dwight D. Eisenhower's solutions were pure Abilene, for the man could not be separated from the boy, and the boy could not be understood apart from his family and his Abilene background. If the town gave him a terribly restricted view of complicated social and economic issues, it also gave him the strength of the steel that is in the English translation of his German name, Eisenhower.

Dwight David Eisenhower was born on October 14, 1890, in Denison, Texas, the third son of David and Ida Eisenhower. When Dwight was two years old the family returned to its earlier home in Abilene, Kansas, where three more sons were born. Arthur was the oldest boy, then came Edgar, Dwight, Roy, Earl, and Milton. Dwight inherited his nickname "Ike" from his two older brothers.

The Eisenhowers lived in a small home on Fourth

An old-fashioned family, photographed in 1902, when Ike was about twelve. Next to Ike (left) *stand Edgar, Earl, Arthur and Roy. David and Ida sit in front with baby Milton.*

Street. They were cramped for living space but they had plenty of room outside, for the house stood on a three-acre tract, complete with a large barn. David Eisenhower was a mechanic and foreman at the Belle Springs Creamery, a milk-processing plant that was the only industry in Abilene. He never had any spare cash, never took a vacation, had no savings, and luxuries were unknown to the Eisenhower family. Nevertheless David and Ida provided food, clothing, shelter, medical care, and most of all, guidance and love, for their six healthy boys.

13

The Eisenhower family took care of most of its own needs. Except for clothes and medicine, plus a few staples such as coffee, salt, and fuel, they raised what they needed in the garden and barn. Everyone helped. Ike could not remember a time when he did not work. The boys rotated jobs. One week Ike would have to get up each morning at 4 A.M. to shovel coal into the furnace to warm the house for the other, later risers; Edgar would milk the cow, while Arthur did the dishes and other housework. Earl would feed the horse while Roy and Milton tended the garden and gathered the eggs. On Sunday, when they got home from church school, the boys cleaned the house and cooked Sunday dinner for the family, while David and Ida attended adult church services. Then on Monday morning the boys shifted jobs, with Ike milking the cow, Earl working in the garden, and so on. Much of the work, especially in the garden, was boring, but it provided the family with nourishing, wholesome food year round—Ida sealed the summer surplus in cans and jars for winter use. And the boys knew that if they didn't work, they wouldn't eat. They learned early to be responsible for their own well-being.

David gave each of his sons a small piece of the garden so that they could earn their own spending money; the boys could raise whatever crops they chose, to sell to the residents of Abilene. They would peddle the vegetables from door to door, pulling them in a wagon or on a cart drawn by the old dray horse. Ike asked around, discovered that sweet corn and cucumbers were the most popular produce, and planted a crop of each. He got two cents for an ear of corn early in the season, one cent per ear later in the year. With about three hundred ears in all to sell, he didn't make much, even in the days when a child could go to the circus for five cents. Still it was something extra which the boys had earned on their own and could be spent as they pleased, and it was enough. Late in his life, Eisenhower recalled that "though our family was far from affluent, I never heard a word even distantly related to self-pity."

Much of the family pride came from Ida, an impressively strong, handsome person who was one of that long line of unsung figures of the American frontier—the women. Born and raised in Virginia, she moved to the Kansas frontier shortly after the Civil War. Like thousands of other women, she somehow managed to bring some comforts to the frontier. She was the rock on which the family rested; from her it drew pride, strength, and courage.

Ida supplied the energy that made the house run. Six days a week David left the house at 7 A.M. and didn't return until 6 P.M. His earnings paid the mortgage, the insurance, the doctor's bills, and bought coal and clothing. Ida managed the garden and the livestock, thereby feeding the family. She also disciplined the boys, except in cases that required severe punishment. Most of all, she set the tone of the household—a tone of fairness, fun, togetherness, discipline, and equality.

She never played favorites or made distinctions between her children, not even after they were grown. Nor did she urge them to compete with each other. Arthur became a banker, Edgar a lawyer, Dwight a soldier, Roy a druggist, Earl an engineer, and Milton an educator. In

1945 when Ike—by then the most famous soldier in the world—was on his way to Abilene for a hero's reception, a reporter said to Ida, "You must be very proud of your son." She looked at the young man, smiled, and replied: "Indeed I am. Which one are you talking about?"

Ida was a deeply religious woman who knew the Bible almost by heart. She was a pacifist, opposed to all war and indeed any kind of violence. But most of all she believed in the fundamentalist Christian doctrine that each person was responsible for his or her own actions. So she didn't interfere, even in a houseful of strong, active boys who could always find something to fight about when there wasn't anything else to do.

Ida's strength, courage, love, and respect for her children were such that no fiction writer would dare invent such a character. When Milton got scarlet fever, the doctor ordered the entire house put under quarantine— no one could enter or leave. David protested that if he missed work for six weeks the family would go into serious debt. Ida said that since she was the only member of the family other than Earl who had been near Milton after he became ill, she and Earl were the only ones who had been exposed. Would it be possible for the doctor to quarantine just her, Earl, and Milton in the bedroom? Then David could go to work and the other boys could continue in school. The doctor agreed, so for six weeks Ida nursed Milton and entertained Earl, never leaving the tiny room. Ike did the cooking and Edgar slid the food in through a crack in the door, which was shut immediately after him. Somehow they all lived through the experience and Milton finally recovered.

A year later, when Ike was in eighth grade, he showed

his own kind of courage. While running home from school he fell and scratched his knee. It wasn't much of a cut; in fact he felt bad only because he had ripped a hole in the new trousers he had just bought with his vegetable earnings. The next day he went to school, but that night the knee began to swell. Blood poisoning had set in. By the time the doctor got there the entire leg below the knee was swollen and black. The doctor drew a line above the knee and advised amputating at that point; he said that only by cutting off Ike's leg above the knee could he save the boy's life.

Ike shook his head. He would not allow it. He said he would rather die than live as a cripple. David and Ida left it up to him—it was his leg and his life.

Each day for the next two weeks the swelling spread. The doctor called in a specialist from Topeka. Both medical men wanted to amputate. Ike still refused.

When the pain became unbearable and he knew he was going to pass out, Ike called Edgar to his side and made him promise that he would never allow them to amputate. "You've got to promise," Ike kept saying. Edgar nodded his solemn agreement. For the next two days and nights Edgar stood guard to keep the doctors away. When the leg was at its worst, all black and swollen to twice its normal size, with a strong-smelling pus oozing from the cut, the doctors told Ida it would be plain and simple murder not to operate. But she left it up to Ike, who was as determined as ever. That night Edgar slept on the threshold of Ike's sickroom door because the feverish Ike was afraid the doctors might try to sneak in and operate.

The next morning the swelling began to subside.

Slowly the fever went down and the blackness faded. The crisis was over. Ike's recovery was slow but complete. Because of the time he missed at school he had to repeat a year. Throughout the entire critical period, one of the Eisenhowers later remembered, Ida in her nightly prayers would of course ask God to help her son, but she also never forgot to plead for the hungry, the unfortunate, and the sick of the world.

Ida was not a person to show her emotions. The boys never saw their father and mother embrace, and Ida didn't do much hugging and kissing of the boys. But they knew of her love and concern, for she showed it in all of her actions.

She had her own, quiet way of soothing hurts and, at the same time, teaching a lesson. The year Ike was ten his father allowed his two older brothers to go out for Halloween "trick or treating." Ike begged and argued, but his parents wouldn't let him go along because he was too young. When Arthur and Edgar left for their fun, Ike rushed outside, tears streaming down his face. He began pounding his fists against the trunk of an old apple tree, hitting it again and again. David finally dragged him away from the tree, gave him a good whipping with a hickory switch, and sent him to bed.

His feelings hurting as much as his behind, his hands a bloody mess, Ike stumbled into bed and for the next hour sobbed into his pillow. Then Ida came into the room, sat in the rocking chair at the foot of the bed, and slowly rocked back and forth. For a long time she didn't say anything. When Ike's sobs were about gone, Ida looked at him and said softly, "He that conquereth his own soul is greater than he who taketh a city," paraphrasing the Bible.

Ida went on to explain that hatred and anger were futile. Ike was only hurting himself. Talking quietly, Ida picked up Ike's hands and began putting salve on them and bandaging the worst places. This helped make the point that his anger had injured no one but himself. Decades later, during his retirement, Eisenhower recalled that conversation "as one of the most valuable moments of my life. . . . To this day I make it a practice to avoid hating anyone." He did indeed. Throughout his army and political careers Eisenhower was known as a person who either said something good about a man or did not mention him at all. He hated no one and simply stayed away from people he did not like.

Nevertheless, Ike had a terrible temper and an awful stubbornness. He took a hundred lickings from Edgar but never gave up and always came back for more. When he entered junior high school the boys from Abilene's south side put him up against the north-side champion in the unofficial annual battle to see which part of town would be supreme in the seventh grade that year. The fight went on for two hours—both boys got bloody noses, torn ears, black eyes, and raw knuckles. Finally the exhausted north-side boy gasped, "I can't lick you." Ike, panting, admitted the same thing and went home. Ida fed him, put him to bed, bandaged his wounds, and said as she closed the door, "I don't like brawling."

In high school, Ike acquired an outlet for his energies. He became one of the town's leading athletes, excelling as an outfielder in baseball and a tackle in football. He was a rawboned kid, all muscle and skinny toughness, weighing 150 pounds, a terror in football and a consistent slap-hitter in baseball. He organized and became president of the Abilene High School Athletic Association; dues from the members provided the money to purchase equipment. Organized sports became the center of his life. Whenever he wasn't working he could usually be found playing one sport or another with his friends.

As a student he was a little above the average. In his freshman year he got 91 in English, 86 in composition, 86 in geography, another 86 in algebra, and 89 in German. Although he never stood at the head of his class, he did do better in his remaining years in high school, especially in history, his favorite subject. Generalities, abstract ideas, and philosophical subjects bored him. He was interested in the immediate and the practical— exact knowledge, facts, solutions. He confined his readings about the past to military history, learning the dates and names of battles, who was in command, how the conflict was waged, who won, and other facts. He knew little and cared less about why the war began or what effect on society it may have had. His heroes were Hannibal and George Washington. His senior yearbook predicted that he would become a professor of history at Yale. The same yearbook predicted that Edgar would be a two-term President of the United States.

Another of Ike's heroes was Bob Davis, a fifty-year-old fisherman, hunter, guide, and poker player. Bob could not read or write but he knew all sorts of fascinating things. Since he had no children of his own, Bob took to Ike, liked to have him around, and taught him all he could—how to hunt ducks, to set a fishnet, to trap musk-rats and mink, to survive alone and unaided in the woods.

Bob gave Ike the individual attention that David could not give him because of David's long working hours. Ida admired Bob Davis and didn't object when Ike spent his weekends at Davis's camp on the Smoky Hill River. Bob taught Ike poker percentages—he would crack Ike's knuckles when the boy went against the percentages by drawing to a four-card straight against an opponent who held openers in five-card draw, jacks or better to open. So thoroughly did Ike learn his lessons that he consistently won in poker until he was forty years old, quitting the game then only because it was embarrassing to take money from his fellow officers and friends. (Eisenhower turned to bridge, but he still stuck to the percentages and became one of the best players in the country.)

The Smoky Hill River, a couple of miles south of Abilene, was the scene of many of Ike's activities. He hunted along its banks, fished in its waters, and organized a number of camping expeditions there. His high-school friends begged him to do the cooking because, thanks to Ida's teaching, he was the only one who knew how to do more than boil an egg. Ike agreed to cook if the others would do all the cleaning up afterward.

The Smoky Hill was usually a quiet little stream, but in spring it sometimes overflowed its banks. In May, 1903, heavy rains west of Abilene sent the Smoky Hill on a rampage. Soon almost all of Abilene was flooded. Buckeye, the main street, was a torrent of water. Abilene's sidewalks were made of wood, and Ike and Edgar found a piece of floating sidewalk big enough to use as a

Ike sits up front, giving out with his famous grin during a fishing and camping trip with friends along the Smoky Hill River.

raft. Along with several friends, the Eisenhower boys started off on a ride down Buckeye toward the river, using their hands to paddle and steer.

They raced down Buckeye, having the time of their lives. They sang songs, blaring forth "Marching Through Georgia" and other old-time favorites. None of the boys noticed that the raft was rapidly floating toward the main riverbed. Once they reached the raging river there would be no chance of keeping the raft upright, and not even a strong man could swim in the roaring current.

Just as the boys were reaching the point of no return a horseman, trying to work his way into Abilene, spotted them. The man rode out to the raft, his horse belly-deep in water, and ordered the boys to get off. They protested, but he insisted. The water was more than waist-deep on the boys, and the footing was slippery, so the horseman stayed behind them to pick up anyone who fell. He herded them back into town like so many cattle.

When Edgar and Ike arrived home, dripping wet, Ida was furious. Not only had they senselessly risked their lives—they had also forgotten to take their father his lunch! Ida hustled them upstairs, stripped off their clothes, took out a maple switch, and gave them the worst whippings of their lives. They hadn't eaten since breakfast, but she sent them to bed without supper.

The next morning Abilene was covered with mud. David put Edgar and Ike to work cleaning off the sidewalks and yard. When they finished, he told them to pump out the basement. David blamed the boys for his flooded basement; they should have stayed home and built small emergency dams around the cellar window openings. The boys worked the pump-wheel the rest of the day. Water poured out of the cellar at a great rate, but every time they checked, the water level seemed as high as ever. It took several days to get it all out. Then David made them clean out all the mud, carrying it from the cellar in buckets. Altogether the backbreaking work took more than a week. The next time there was a flood Ike and Edgar stayed home and built such excellent dams that not a drop of water got into the cellar.

There never was any doubt in the Eisenhower household about where final authority rested—it was with David. A quiet man who had seen his share of troubles (he had once been half-owner of a grocery store, but his partner ran off with the money and left him bankrupt), he nevertheless impressed on his boys the promise of American life. Opportunity lies all around you, he told them; all you have to do is reach out and take it. He insisted on total honesty and would not allow quibbling or little white lies. To observers David seemed a cold man who had little time, or even love, for his children. The boys felt differently. David may not have shown them his love in any obvious way, but they were always confident that it was there.

In 1942 when David died, Ike wrote a note to himself in an attempt to describe his feelings about his father. "He was a just man," Ike wrote, "well liked, well educated, a thinker. He was undemonstrative, quiet, modest, and of exemplary habits—he never used alcohol or tobacco. He was an uncomplaining person in the face of adversity, and such plaudits as were accorded him did not inflate his ego." There was more. Ike felt that David's "finest monument" was his reputation in Abilene. "His word has been his bond and accepted as such; his sterling honesty, his insistence upon the immediate payment of all debts, his pride in his independence earned for him a reputation that has profited all of us boys."

Summing up, Ike declared, "I'm proud he was my father! My only regret is that it was always so difficult to let him know the great depth of my affection for him."

In 1909 Ike graduated from high school. He wanted to go to college, not so much because he was ambitious, but because he wanted to continue his promising football and baseball careers. But David could not afford to pay for a college education, even for one boy, and Edgar hoped to become a lawyer. So Edgar and Ike worked out a deal. "We both want to go," Ike said, "but you know what you want to do, and I don't. Besides, you're the oldest, so you ought to go first. Why don't I stay out next year and work and send you all the extra money I make? Then the next year you stay out and work and send me the money you make. We can take college work on alternate years that way and both end up with college educations."

Edgar gladly agreed. After working that summer in the creamery, he went off in the fall to the University of Michigan. Ike held a number of jobs that year, ending up as night foreman at the creamery, and he managed to send Edgar more than two hundred dollars. The only luxury he allowed himself was a few dollars for shotgun shells.

During the course of the year Ike became close friends with Swede Hazlett, the son of one of Abilene's physicians. Swede was spending the year studying for the entrance examination for the United States Naval Academy at Annapolis. He urged Ike to seek an appointment too so they could stay together.

Ike thought it a marvelous dream. The Naval Academy played a big-time college football schedule and, even better, offered a free college education. But the only way to get in was through appointment, and he doubted that any Kansas congressman would give him one, because his family had no political influence. Swede convinced him to try, so Ike went calling on the important business and professional men in Abilene, asking them to write to Senator Bristow. Thanks to David's reputation throughout the county, everyone Ike called on agreed to write a recommendation.

Senator Bristow was impressed by the glowing recommendations of Ike from men whose judgment he trusted. He arranged for a competitive examination. Ike would take the test along with half a dozen other candidates—the boy who ranked highest would get the appointment.

Ike and Swede spent the next few months studying together, six hours and more a day. In addition, Ike went back to high school to take advanced courses in science and mathematics. He also continued to hold a full-time night job at the creamery and send money to Edgar.

When Ike took the test he felt he had done well, but there was no way to tell for sure. Then he got some bad news. He was twenty-one years old—a year beyond the Annapolis age limit. He was ready to forget the whole dream, when Bristow informed him that he had placed first and the Senator had decided to appoint him to West Point instead.

Ike had not given a thought to West Point before, but it seemed a good idea. After all, Army played football too, and the education was also free there. He doubled his study efforts to insure success in the West Point entrance examination. In the spring of 1911 he went to St. Louis, took the examination, and passed. Come June, he would be a cadet at the United States Military Academy at West Point. After that he would be a soldier. Neither David nor Ida tried to stop him, even though by becoming a soldier he was going against their deep pacifist beliefs. Ida merely said, "It's your choice," and kept her feelings to herself. She went alone to her room and cried. Milton later told his brother that was the only time he ever heard their mother cry.

In early June of 1911 Ike set off for West Point; he was a grown man, strong, self-confident, capable. By later standards he was woefully uneducated—the Abilene school system had taught him to read and write, some mathematics, a little science, a smattering of historical dates without any significant interpretation of events, and not much else. It had been enough to enable him to pass the examination, but no more. He had no sense of the clouds of World War I then gathering over Europe, and only the barest knowledge of international relations. Nor did he have more than a dim idea of America's national problems. The Progressive movement, then at its peak throughout the United States, hardly touched him at all; he knew nothing about the problems stemming from America's rapid industrialization, nor about racism and its consequences. Like most people in Abilene, he took it for granted that the North had fulfilled its obligations to black people by freeing them from slavery during the

Civil War. His political views, in short, were commonplace, reflecting nothing more than majority sentiment in Abilene. He accepted without question the little he had been taught about the outside world.

But if he was uninformed about the broad social, economic, and political issues of the day, he did know himself, and that was more important. On the streets of Abilene, in its schools and on its playgrounds, and most of all from his parents, he had discovered himself. He knew what he could do and realized that he had a solid foundation on which to build. Far from fearing the future, he anticipated it. His good health, powerful muscles, self-discipline, ability to get things done—all these characteristics helped. But the key to his confidence was his happiness. Abilene had been a good place to grow up. The young man who climbed on the Union Pacific Railroad for the ride east to West Point was supremely happy. He liked himself and enjoyed life. And he was confident that he could handle anything the world might throw his way.

chapter three
West Point

The United States Military Academy at West Point is situated on the banks of the Hudson River, upriver from New York City. It had once been America's leading scientific college, but civilian schools had surpassed it after the Civil War, and when Ike became a cadet the Academy was, at best, only an average engineering college. Still, it retained its worldwide reputation for tough discipline. Because it was tuition-free, because its students were appointed by congressmen from among numerous applicants, and also because of its rigid entrance examination, each June the Academy received some of the best young men in the country. Most came from small towns, where they had been the outstanding athletes or scholars or both. These young men were cocky, sure of themselves, boastful. In their view, West Point was lucky to have them.

The West Point system was designed to cut them down

to size. Every day, in every possible way, West Point's officials and its older cadets taught the entering cadets—called "plebes"—that they were little pieces of nothing, mere fluff that would blow away on a slight breeze and never be missed. Eisenhower once recalled that the first thing a plebe learned was that he was "awkward, clumsy, and of unequaled stupidity." Older cadets would order the plebe into a stiff attention, then ask a nonsensical question. When the tormented plebe could not answer, the cadet would shout insulting remarks at him, berate him for his ignorance, remind him that there was nothing in the world lower than a plebe, and then order fifty or one hundred push-ups for failure to answer the question. During the summer the cadets lived in tents; plebes were likely to find their tent stakes pulled up during the night, or to have the poles removed and the canvas collapse on top of them. They were sent on long, fruitless errands. They were ordered to march in formation, then made fun of because they could not keep in step. Everything had to be done at double-time. Pick up those clothes! Bring in that bedding! Take down that tent! Put up that tent!

The aim of the system was not only to deflate a few swelled heads, but also to develop unquestioning, immediate obedience, hopefully without breaking the plebe's spirit. The Academy's sole purpose was to turn

A practice punt on West Point's football field. Ike might have been an All-American halfback, but an injury during his sophomore year ended that dream.

out junior Army officers who would see themselves as a part of the whole rather than as individuals seeking self-glory. West Point sought to create a team without stars.

Many plebes could not stand the humiliation or refused to accept the restraints on their personal freedom. They either left in disgust or the system broke them and they were forced to go. Ike stayed. He didn't particularly like the hazing, but he was older than his fellow plebes and in much better physical condition, so all the double-timing and extra work didn't bother him. His ego was secure enough to allow him to laugh at the insults—at least to himself. Moreover he could see the point to the hazing—he realized it was part of a system designed to make him into a soldier, and he accepted it.

Ike was proud to be a cadet. At the end of his first day at the Point, all the plebes gathered together to take the oath of allegiance. As he raised his right hand to repeat the oath he was swept by the feeling that the words "United States of America" would have a new meaning for him; from that moment on it would be the nation he would serve, not himself. "Across half a century," he wrote in his memoirs, "I can look back and see a rawboned, gawky Kansas boy from the farm country, earnestly repeating the words that would make him a cadet."

Ike's pride in being a cadet, even if a lowly plebe, helped him survive the hazing. So did his sense of humor. Many of West Point's rules and regulations were, quite simply, absurd—especially those that gave older cadets the right to order plebes around. One day Cadet Corporal Thomas Adler caught Ike and another plebe named Atkins in a minor infraction of regulations. Adler ordered the offenders to report to his room after tattoo in "full-dress coats," meaning in complete uniform. Ike and Atkins, however, decided to have a little fun of their own and obey the literal words of the order.

The full-dress coat had a long tail in back, a glittering row of buttons in front. When the appointed time came, Ike and Atkins marched into Adler's room wearing the coats—but nothing else. They snapped to attention, saluted with a flourish, and declared: "Sir, Cadets Eisenhower and Atkins reporting as ordered."

It was an old gag—Edgar Allan Poe had used it when he was a cadet before the Civil War—but it was effective. Corporal Adler roared his anger. Other upperclassmen in the room roared with laughter, laughter directed at Adler, not Eisenhower and Atkins. The plebes had to pay a price—Adler had them stand at attention for hours, with their backs, heads, buttocks, and bare legs pressed against the wall ("bracing"). But they still enjoyed the joke at Adler's expense.

Ike adjusted to the West Point system by making fun of it when he could, and accepting it when he had to. He did what he was told—or at least enough of what he was told to remain a cadet in good standing. After his first year he was no longer a plebe, and upperclassmen could not harass him, but Army officers could and did hand out bad-conduct marks for breaking the rules. If a cadet received too many demerits he was dismissed from the Academy. If he stayed below the dismissal number he was still punished by being forced to spend his Sunday afternoons marching back and forth on the parade ground, carrying a rifle on his shoulder.

Ike spent most of his Sundays marching, for offenses were possible everywhere—dust on the window sills of the cadet's room, being late for formation, an unbuttoned jacket, or unpolished shoes. Ike kept his room and his clothes just neat enough to avoid dismissal, but not neat enough to avoid constant demerits. After his four years at West Point he stood 125th in discipline, out of a class of 162. He lived by the rules, more or less, but he did not allow the system to destroy his fun-loving independence.

Nor did he lose his sense of fair play. Many plebes, having survived the first year, turned into holy terrors when the next class of plebes came to the Point. Indeed most hazing was done by sophomores who had sworn during their plebe year that they would "get" the next class. They made every effort to outdo their own tormentors of the previous season, and the truth is that they often went too far—suicides among plebes were not unknown at West Point.

In his sophomore year Ike indulged in such harassment, until one day when he was knocked down by a frightened, breathless plebe who was rushing around the parade ground trying to carry out an impossible order. Pretending great indignation, Ike picked himself up and demanded to know what the stupid animal lying before him had done in civilian life. Scornfully, Ike added, "You look like a barber."

The plebe, deeply flushed, replied: "I was a barber, sir."

Ike went to his tent and told his roommate, "I'm never going to crawl another plebe as long as I live. As a matter of fact, they'll have to run over and knock me out of the company street before I'll make any attempt again. I've just done something that was stupid and unforgivable. I managed to make a man ashamed of the work he did to earn a living." Never again did Ike haze a plebe.

West Point's discipline was something Ike learned to live with, but he had not come to the Academy to learn to obey orders. He had two major goals—to be an athlete, and to get a free college education. During his plebe year, football and baseball were the center of his life. Unfortunately, although he was five feet eleven inches tall, he weighed only 152 pounds, so despite his hard muscles he was too light for varsity football. He did play with the scrubs, where his determination brought him to the attention of the coach, and he resolved to gain weight and work on his speed before the next season began. In baseball he was a chop-hitter, poking the ball to all corners of the field. The West Point coach told him that he was a good fielder and might play on the team next year if he would start swinging freely at the ball.

All summer, whenever he could find some spare time, Ike practiced hitting and worked on the track in an effort to improve his speed. At every meal he ate until he almost burst. When the 1912 football season began he had built up his weight to 174 pounds, had picked up some speed, and showed more guts than anyone on the Army team. He quickly became one of the star halfbacks. After the first few games, newspapers began to mention his name as a possible All-American.

During a midseason game against Tufts, Ike took the snap from center, plunged through the line, broke clear, and started for the goal line. A Tufts halfback dove at him and caught his foot. Ike spun—and twisted his knee. The joint swelled rapidly and he had to be carried from the field and sent to the hospital. He was sick at the thought of missing the big game of the year against Navy, which was coming up in two weeks. After the swelling went down he left the hospital, seemingly cured, and with a promise that he could play against Navy the next year.

Then a few days later he was doing "monkey drill" in the riding hall—leaping off and on his galloping horse. He hit the ground hard, the recently injured knee buckled under him, and he couldn't get up. He had torn the cartilages and tendons, and spent the next month on his back in the hospital. His athletic career was over. For the rest of his life he had to favor the knee, and never again did he run at full speed.

Ike was terribly depressed. Nothing could cheer him up. He would never again play football or baseball for Army; half his reason for coming to West Point was gone. He thought about quitting the Academy, and on a number of occasions his roommate had to talk him out of resigning. Only the fact of a free education kept him going. Eventually his spirits lifted a little, especially after the Army coach assigned him to coach the scrubs. Ike became an excellent football coach; after graduation he was much in demand to coach at the Army's posts and forts. He also became a cheerleader at the Academy. But he never realized his dream of playing against Navy.

In one sense it is impossible to exaggerate the importance of the knee injury. Ike had dedicated his life to athletics and in a single stroke all that was taken away from him. He had nothing to replace it with. He might have directed his ambition into other areas, but he was not particularly keen on becoming a soldier and had no inclination to become a scholar. He might have quit the Academy, gone home to Abilene, taken work in the creamery, played a little poker, done some hunting, and lived out his life as an unknown Kansan.

But he would not allow the crisis to defeat him, even though it did not spur him to greater scholarly or military efforts. Instead, he ignored it and carried on as usual. He still had more than his share of fun and got more than his share of demerits. He still did enough to get by in the classroom, but nowhere near enough to become a top scholar. His roommate said of him, "Poor Dwight merely consents to exist until graduation shall set him free. At one time he threatened to get interested in life and won his 'A' by being the most promising back in Eastern football—but the Tufts game broke his knee and the promise."

In the classroom, as in matters of discipline, Ike did no more than enough. He usually stood just above the middle in the scholastic ranking of his class. In his senior year, for example, out of 164 men in his class he was 59th in civil and military engineering, 82nd in ordnance and gunnery, 45th in law, 72nd in Spanish, and 57th in practical military engineering. Overall he stood 61st in his class.

In an official report an officer judged Ike to be an average cadet. "We saw in Eisenhower a not uncommon type," the officer said. "A man who would thoroughly enjoy his army life, giving both to duty and recreation their fair values, but we did not see in him a man who would throw himself into a job so completely that nothing else would matter." As the officers at the Academy saw him, there was "nothing outstanding" about Ike.

His classmates thought differently. Ike was extremely popular: he was so natural, so loose, and most of all, so considerate of other people's feelings and so fair in his dealings. In addition to his cheerleading and coaching, Ike participated in a variety of activities and came to know most of his fellow cadets well. Omar Bradley, a classmate, became one of his close friends. Ike was highly impressed by Bradley and wrote of him in the school yearbook, "Brad's most important characteristic is 'getting there,' and if he keeps up the clip he's started some of us will someday be bragging that, 'Sure, General Bradley was a classmate of mine.' "

No one predicted that Ike would become a general. He did make cadet corporal once, but was busted back to private for excessive demerits. Still, when Swede Hazlett visited West Point, he was not surprised to find Ike "generally liked and admired. Had he not indulged in so many extracurricular activities he could easily have led his class scholastically. Everyone was his friend— but with no loss in dignity or respect."

So Ike got through West Point with a creditable record. He learned a great many practical facts at the Academy, but when he graduated he knew only a little more history, philosophy, literature, and political science than he had learned at Abilene High School. Even though he had a college diploma, he was not what could be called a well-educated man.

Cadet Eisenhower frowns for his graduation mug shot.

Neither was he highly motivated. West Point tries, usually successfully, to make a deep impression on its cadets, to inspire them to serve their country as soldiers to the best of their abilities. Few men go through West Point without having its stamp put on them. Ike was one of the minority—he put in his four years there, but it was not a crucial time in his life. He got his education and made lasting friendships, but that was all.

West Point attempts to make its cadets *want* to be soldiers; with Ike it did not succeed. On the eve of his graduation he was told that because of his bad knee, Army regulations would prevent him from receiving his officer's commission. Such news would have disturbed most cadets, but Ike merely shrugged and wrote for information on Argentina. He was curious about the gauchos, and Argentina sounded to him a little like the Old West, so he thought he would go down there for a couple of years and try his hand at being a cowboy. It seemed as good a choice as any.

Fortunately, the Army doctor relented; he told Ike he could have a commission if he would promise to apply for the Infantry, where his bad knee wouldn't hamper him as much as it would in the Cavalry. Ike liked horses and would have chosen the Cavalry, but under the circumstances, he decided the Infantry would do. So, somewhat reluctantly, in June, 1915, he became Second Lieutenant Dwight David Eisenhower, U.S. Army, Infantry. He had no dreams of glory, but figured that life as an Army officer would be as good as anything else he could think of.

chapter four

A Period of Preparation (1915–1929)

West Point had taught Eisenhower how to be a good second lieutenant. Over the next fifteen years the Army taught him how to be a good senior officer. These were full and satisfying years for Ike—years in which he fell in love, married, took on the responsibilities of being a father, and matured as a human being. His personal growth complemented his growth as a soldier. He became interested in his profession and, thanks to the Army's postgraduate school system, some inspired teaching, and the nature of his assignments, became a recognized expert in his field.

The growth, however, was limited. An Army officer lived a life that was more like a monk's than anything else. During these years Ike had little contact with civilians, and those he did meet were highly placed, powerful men who were not representative of the bulk of the American public. He remained ignorant of the great social and political issues of the day, hardly aware of the conditions under which poor people and members of minority groups lived. Because of his ignorance he changed few of his political views, which remained as conservative as those voiced on Main Street, Abilene. (By way of contrast, his younger brother Milton became a famous educator and one of the foremost liberals in the Republican Party.)

The Army took care of all of Ike's wants. His family had free medical service, he always had a home provided for him, he enjoyed total security (except for a court-martial, he could never be fired), and in general lived in an all-protective world. Later, when he became President and denounced socialism and the so-called welfare state, critics pointed out that even the most advanced socialist country did not give its citizens the kind of protection and care he had received as an Army officer. He simply had no idea of the kinds of difficulties most people have in trying to earn their daily bread or in keeping a roof over their heads. So while he grew, gradually abandoning his interest in football and poker but increasing and deepening his fascination with military history, he remained politically unaware. He never voted and refused to discuss politics with anyone. He thought of himself as a simple soldier.

In the beginning of his career Eisenhower was not a serious student of war. His real interest during his early years in the Army was an affair of the heart.

Eisenhower's first assignment was to the 19th Infantry Regiment in San Antonio, Texas, in the fall of 1915. The duty was routine and Ike usually finished work before noon. He spent much of his free time hunting, but poker was his great passion. He played at every opportunity and he usually won, making enough money to pay off the debts incurred in purchasing his first set of uniforms. He also coached the football team. But although he was a handsome bachelor with a big, winning grin, he spent no time courting any of the unmarried young women of San Antonio.

One Sunday afternoon in October, a month or so after he arrived in San Antonio, Eisenhower was serving as officer of the day, walking around the post on an inspection tour. The wife of Major Hunter Harris of the 19th Infantry, standing in a group of visitors, called to him, "Ike, won't you come over here? I have some people I'd like you to meet."

"Sorry, Mrs. Harris," Eisenhower called back. "I'm on guard and have to stand an inspection tour."

Mrs. Harris muttered to a young woman standing beside her, "There goes the woman-hater of the post." To the young woman, Eisenhower had been just another second lieutenant, but Mrs. Harris's remark had made him an object of some interest. She urged Mrs. Harris to ask again.

"We didn't ask you to come over to *stay*," Mrs. Harris called out. "Just come over here and meet these friends of mine." Eisenhower agreed that he could do that much and walked across the street, where he met the Doud family of Denver. But after a polite exchange of greetings, he had eyes only for the daughter, a small, attractive girl who was, in Ike's words, "saucy in the look about her face and in her whole attitude." He was so taken by the eighteen-year-old Mamie Geneva Doud that he asked her if she would accompany him on his rounds of the guard posts. To his astonishment, Mamie agreed.

For Eisenhower, it was love at first sight. For Mamie, it was something less. Ike was fun enough, but the Douds had been spending their winters at San Antonio for years and she had dozens of boyfriends around the post. She enjoyed the walk, then forgot it.

The next day when Mamie returned from an all-day picnic, the maid told her that a "Mr. I-something" had been calling every fifteen minutes all afternoon, asking for her. Just then the phone rang again. It was that same "Mr. I-something," formally asking "Miss Doud" if she would go dancing with him that evening. She was sorry, but she already had a date. What about the next night? She had a date for that night too. Well, how about the big dance at the Majestic that week? Mamie laughed and said she wouldn't be free for the dance at the Majestic for four weeks.

"All right, then," Ike said calmly, "how about four weeks from now?" Somewhat overwhelmed, Mamie accepted. Over the course of the following winter Ike spent more and more time with Mamie and her family, becoming close friends with her parents and falling deeply in love with Mamie. She tried to keep their relationship casual, for she thoroughly enjoyed being the most popular unmarried girl in San Antonio, dating different lieutenants every night. But gradually Ike eliminated the competition.

The Douds' home in Denver was only a few hundred miles from Abilene, but there was a vast difference between Mamie's and Ike's families, primarily because the Douds were wealthy. They liked Ike well enough but were afraid that Mamie, accustomed to having maids, big houses, and money for luxuries, would be miserable trying to live on a lieutenant's pay. But she was slowly falling in love with this big, strong Kansan who was so direct in everything he did. She was a strong-willed person herself and she decided she wanted to spend the rest of her life with Ike, whatever the hardships. When he proposed marriage, she accepted.

Complications ensued. Bored with the deadly routine of the infantry post, Ike had applied for transfer to the Aviation Section of the Army—he figured that being a flier would be more exciting than being in an infantry unit. The day after Mr. Doud gave his blessing to the marriage, Eisenhower learned that his application had been approved and he was ordered to report to the post hospital for a physical examination. He ran over to the Douds' house to tell them the good news—not only would he have a more exciting career, he would also receive fifty percent more pay.

But when he told the Douds, a deep silence filled their living room. Finally Mr. Doud said that he had been ready to welcome Ike into the family, but if he were so irresponsible as to go into the flying business, he would have to reconsider. Flying, he said, was far too risky for a young man with a new wife to care for. The Douds didn't want Mamie to become a widow in her youth. The wedding would have to be called off.

Ike plunged from elation to depression. He walked home slowly. For two days he thought about his choice—

the glamor of flying versus marriage to Mamie. Then he called the Douds and informed them that he had withdrawn his application for the Aviation Section. Relieved and delighted, they began preparations for the wedding, which took place in Denver on July 1, 1916. The same day, Eisenhower was promoted to first lieutenant.

That night Mamie and Ike took the train from Denver to Abilene, where the Eisenhowers would meet their daughter-in-law for the first time. The newlyweds arrived at 4 A.M., but Ida and David were up to greet them. Ida took Mamie in her arms and said she had always wanted to have a daughter and now was proud to have such a fine-looking one. David gave her a warm welcome. Mamie, who had been terrified at the prospect of meeting her husband's family, began laughing and chatting gaily with her new parents-in-law. When Earl and Milton came downstairs she gave them each a hug and told them how happy she was to finally have some brothers. Ida put out a huge fried-chicken breakfast, for the young couple had to catch a noon train back to San Antonio.

A few weeks later Ike took Mamie back to Abilene so she could spend some time with his family. One afternoon, right after lunch, he announced that he was going to see the old gang. Mamie said that was fine since she had so much to talk about with Ida.

At suppertime he had not returned. "What do you suppose can have happened to him?" Mamie asked. "Nothing serious," Ida replied. "He's probably in a poker game with his friends down at the café." Mamie said nothing. At supper she was too furious to eat. When darkness fell he still had not returned. Mamie couldn't stand it. She called the café.

Bride and groom, Ike and Mamie Doud Eisenhower, on their wedding day. Ike has just been commissioned second lieutenant.

He spoke before she could, telling her he was sorry to be late, but he was losing money and he never left a poker game while he was behind. His easy explanation and calm tone made Mamie angrier than ever.

"You come home this minute."

"Now, now, Mamie, I've just explained. It's against my principles to quit when I'm licked. It won't be long—"

"If you don't come home this minute you needn't bother to come at all," Mamie stormed, slamming down the receiver.

He didn't come. Instead he went back to the game, played until 2 A.M., when he was well ahead, and came home singing. Mamie met him at the door. What happened then only Mamie and Ike knew; all that either of them would say afterward was that it was their biggest, longest, and most serious fight. Ike learned that his bride had even more spirit than he had thought; Mamie learned that her man had an extremely strong will. Each came to respect the other's position more than ever and they emerged from the quarrel more deeply in love than before.

During the past three years, from 1914 to 1917, the bloodiest war in history had been tearing Europe apart. The German Army had thrown itself against the Russian, British, and French Armies. Gigantic battles, stretching over tens of miles and lasting for months, left hundreds of thousands dead and wounded. Yet Eisenhower had paid almost no attention to it, for like most Americans he assumed that the United States would never be involved, and he was not interested enough in warfare to spend time studying the events of World War I.

The war did not affect him until the beginning of 1917, when President Woodrow Wilson began to increase the size of the U.S. Army as a way of preparing for possible American entry into the war. Now Eisenhower found himself assigned to a recruiting camp about twenty miles outside San Antonio, where he and Mamie had their small living quarters.

In April, 1917, after the Germans began sinking American ships carrying war goods to England, the United States declared war on Germany. Like most soldiers, the twenty-six-year-old Eisenhower wanted to get overseas immediately, to the scene of combat in France. He had been trained for war, and besides, promotions came faster to those in combat than to those stuck with training duty in the States. But though Eisenhower made constant application for transfer to a combat unit, he had no luck—he was sent to Georgia as a staff officer at a training camp. There, he got into trouble with his commanding officer because of his almost daily applications for transfer. Finally he got orders to go to Camp Meade, Maryland, to join a tank battalion just being organized. Tanks were a new weapon—they had been used by the British for the first time only a year earlier—and they were almost as exciting as airplanes. Eisenhower was delighted, especially since the unit was scheduled to go overseas as soon as it was equipped and trained.

The unit went to France, but Eisenhower was not with it. His superiors were so impressed with his organizational and training ability that they sent him, instead, to

Camp Colt in Gettysburg, Pennsylvania, to train volunteers for the Tank Corps. Eisenhower was bitterly disappointed—his classmates were in France, winning promotions and medals daily, while he was stuck with stateside duty. There was a challenge involved, however, and he did his best to meet it. He learned everything he could about tanks and their use in war, trained the men, and meanwhile bombarded the War Department with requests for transfer to France.

Ike was unhappy at being stuck in the States, but there was a good side to it. Mamie had just had her first child. The baby boy was named Doud Dwight, called "Icky" for short. Mamie then joined her husband in Gettysburg. A professional soldier spends long periods separated from his family because often the family can't join him on his assignment, so Ike was especially pleased to be with his wife and son right after the birth. The new father was terribly proud of his son and showered love and affection on him. A warmhearted and generous man, Ike enjoyed playing with Icky, hugging and kissing him, and watching Mamie take care of the boy. He really enjoyed just being around his family.

But he still wanted overseas combat duty. In September, 1918, Eisenhower went to see a general in the War Department who told him that if he would agree to give up his application for overseas service he would be promoted to full colonel and put in charge of a large training camp. Eisenhower declined. He was ready to take a reduction in rank, he said, if he could just get overseas. He was not interested in promotion.

In October his orders finally came. He was to move the

Tank Corps to New York for immediate shipment to the combat zone in Europe. By the time he arrived in New York, however, the Germans had signed the Armistice and the war was over. Eisenhower had missed his chance. He was still a captain when most of his classmates were majors and some were colonels. President Wilson had said that the war was a war to end all wars, so there did not seem much future for a young Army officer. Eisenhower thought about resigning and taking up a civilian occupation.

He decided to stay in the Army after he got orders to report to Camp Meade, where he could continue his work with tanks. The new weapon was clumsy and tended to break down at critical moments, but Eisenhower was convinced that it would be improved and become the dominant weapon of future wars—if there ever were any. Like the pilots of the time, tank officers were ridiculed by men in the Infantry or Cavalry, who couldn't understand why anyone would waste his time with such fool inventions. The pilots and tankers, in turn, regarded themselves as prophets, representing the wave of the future. At Meade, Eisenhower met other young soldiers who also believed in the future of tanks, including some who had had experience with tank warfare in France.

Chief among these was Colonel George S. Patton, Jr., with whom Eisenhower immediately struck up a close friendship. Together, they explored the possibilities of tanks and studied their potential use in battle. The two men could not have been more different—Eisenhower was solid, Patton was flashy; Eisenhower was poor, Patton was extremely wealthy. Eisenhower believed in thorough planning and was concerned with supplies and the other mundane matters pertaining to support for the fighting line; Patton believed in dash and style, maintaining that a tank unit with good morale would break through enemy lines whatever the plans or supply situation. Despite their differences, or perhaps because of them, the two men were constantly together, constantly learning from each other. They made a perfect team.

Icky, meanwhile, had become Ike's daily companion. When Icky was two, his father discovered that the boy loved parades with military music, so he took him to the parade ground at the end of each day to watch the men march past. "I was inclined to display Icky and his talents at the slightest excuse, or without one," Ike later confessed. The enlisted men were fond of Icky; they got together and bought him a tank uniform, including overcoat and overseas cap. Whenever they went out on a tank drill, one of the men would stop off at the Eisenhowers' to pick up Icky. They would put him in the tank and treat him as one of the boys.

In the summer of 1920 Eisenhower went on a special assignment—"through darkest America with tank and truck," as he described it later. The Army decided to send a convoy of all types of motor vehicles across the United States—vehicles which were then being adopted for regular use in the Army. This was done partly for publicity purposes, partly to dramatize the need for better highways. Hardly any of the roads were paved and few were graded; most were unbearably dusty in dry weather and became impassable mudholes when it rained. The convoy averaged sixty miles per ten-hour day. Eisenhower took advantage of the journey to learn as much as he could about the country, most of which he was seeing for the first time.

Practical jokes helped pass the time. Once Ike and some other officers from the western states convinced some of the easterners (who were a little frightened at finding themselves in the great American West) that an Indian uprising was expected. The easterners stood guard duty all night. Another day Ike shot a jackrabbit with his .22 rifle. A friend set the dead animal up against a tree, about a thousand yards from the road. In the evening Ike and his friend, along with some easterners, rode past the scene. The friend pointed to the jackrabbit, which in the fading light could barely be seen, and called out, "Ike, why don't you take a crack at him? You're the finest pistol shot I've ever seen." Ike whipped out his pistol, pointed it in the general direction of the rabbit, and fired.

"You've got him! You've got him! He fell!" the friend shouted, running toward the rabbit. He brought it back about halfway so that the easterners could see it, then threw the long-dead rabbit into the brush where it couldn't be examined. When the hoodwinked easterners protested, Ike said the jackrabbit was too stringy to eat and not worth bringing in.

If playing jokes was typical of Ike, so too was his reluctance to hurt anyone needlessly. He and his friend had planned to tell the easterners about the practical jokes, but when Ike realized that they had been completely taken in by the Indian, rabbit, and other pranks, and would be terribly hurt if they discovered these were all jokes, he decided to keep his mouth shut and not embarrass them.

Shortly after Ike returned to Camp Meade, three-year-old Icky got scarlet fever. The camp doctor called in specialists, but Icky continued to get worse. Ike couldn't even be with his son because scarlet fever is highly contagious, but there was a porch at the hospital from which he could wave to Icky. Hour after hour, Ike and Mamie haunted the halls of the hospital. All they could do was hope and pray. It was not enough. In late December, 1920, Icky died.

It was a terrible blow. Even half a century later, when he wrote his memoirs, Ike winced at the memory. "This was the greatest disappointment and disaster in my life," he wrote, "the one I have never been able to forget completely. Today when I think of it, even now as I write of it, the keenness of our loss comes back to me as fresh and as terrible as it was in that long dark day soon after Christmas, 1920. My wife and I have arranged that when it comes our time to be buried, to be laid away in our final resting place, we shall have him with us." As for Mamie, Ike wrote, "the loss was heartbreaking, and her grief in turn would have broken the hardest heart."

Ike drifted through the days in a haze; he found it difficult to concentrate or get interested in anything. He did his job without enthusiasm. Slowly, ever so slowly, the Eisenhowers recovered from their grief.

Then in January, 1922, a few months after his thirty-first birthday, Ike got the biggest break of his young career. He was ordered to the Panama Canal Zone, to serve at Camp Gaillard as executive officer to General

Fox Connor. Connor was one of those great men who never have the opportunity to prove themselves. In World War I he had served as General John J. Pershing's operations officer in charge of all planning, and Pershing regarded him as one of the best younger officers in the Army. But he was too young for a high command in World War I, and by the time World War II came he was too old and had retired from active duty. Still, he influenced most of the famous American generals of World War II, especially Eisenhower.

Connor was not merely a soldier; he was also a philosopher and a student of military history. He and Eisenhower had to ride horseback from outpost to outpost in the Canal Zone; when they made camp at night they sat around the fire and discussed the campaigns of the Civil War or Napoleon's battles. Eisenhower had not given much thought to military history over the preceding years; the reason was, in his words, "its treatment at West Point as an out-and-out memory course. . . . Little attempt was made to explain the meaning of a battle, why it came about, what the commanders hoped to accomplish." If this was military history, Eisenhower had concluded, he "wanted no part of it."

Connor reawakened his interest by asking probing questions: "What would you have done on the second day at Gettysburg if you had been Lee?" or "What would have happened if Grant had done just the opposite of what he did?" Connor forced Eisenhower to think about what he was reading, to think about war. Soon Connor had Eisenhower reading the military philosophers such as Karl von Clausewitz, Ardant du Picq, Dennis Mahan, and Ferdinand Foch. By directing his reading and by questioning him, Connor gave Eisenhower a postgraduate education in military affairs.

Their talks around the campfire ranged far afield. Connor liked to hand down axioms such as "Always take your job seriously, never yourself," or "All generalities are false, including this one." He told Eisenhower that another world war was inevitable, that the United States would have to fight in both Asia and Europe as part of an alliance, and that the key to victory would be getting the allies to work together for a common cause. Connor urged Eisenhower to get to know Colonel George Marshall, who Connor said was a true genius and a sure bet to be the United States Army Chief of Staff in the next war. Years later, when Eisenhower was a retired President of the United States and had worked with nearly all the great men of the century, he recalled those campfire talks and declared, "Fox Connor was the ablest man I ever knew."

Under Connor's direction, Eisenhower found a sense of purpose. For the first time he became a serious student of his profession, which he found to his delight was truly interesting and exciting. When Swede Hazlett's submarine stopped for repairs at the Canal Zone, Swede spent a few days with Ike. He noted that Eisenhower was working and studying hard, even though "this was particularly unusual at a torrid, isolated post where most officers spent their off hours trying to keep cool and amused." Eisenhower had charge of planning for the defense of the Canal Zone in case of attack, and he explained his plans to Swede "with the enthusiasm of genius." Still, for all his hard work, Eisenhower was "no studious recluse—he missed none of the fun, he never did."

In August, 1922, Mamie's second son was born. They named him John and he quickly became, Ike later recalled, "a walking, talking, running-the-whole-household young fellow." John did much to fill the gap left by the death of Icky. As Ike put it, "Living in the present with a healthy, bouncing baby boy can take parents' minds off almost anything."

When Eisenhower's two-year tour at the Canal Zone was finished he had short assignments at posts in Georgia and Colorado. Connor, meanwhile, was using his many connections with the top brass in Washington, D.C., to get Eisenhower appointed to the Command and General Staff College, in Leavenworth, Kansas. C&GS was a postgraduate school for majors and above, designed to train promising young officers for eventual higher command. It had a great deal of prestige; no one could hope to advance above the rank of lieutenant colonel without having gone through the Leavenworth course.

Students at Leavenworth were ranked according to the level of their performance, and competition was intense. The students were under so much pressure that almost every year one or more men broke down and committed suicide. Men who graduated near the top of their class, on the other hand, greatly enhanced their reputations and could expect choice assignments in the future. If West Point was the testing ground for the officer corps, C&GS was the testing ground for higher command.

Eisenhower approached his year at Leavenworth with

A 1925 front-porch reunion in Abilene. Behind: *Roy, Arthur, Earl, Edgar and Milton. David and Ida sit with Ike, who's home on leave.*

more seriousness than he had felt for any other job. For months before the class began he pored over previous C&GS problems. He was soon an expert at arriving at the right answers to tactical and strategic questions. When he began the formal course of study, in August, 1925, he stepped up the pace. Mamie later recalled that year as one during which she never saw her husband. Each night he went upstairs to a quiet room and pored over

58

his books; each day he attended classes or read. The work paid off. On graduation day, in a class of 275, Eisenhower stood first. It was a major triumph. Throughout the Army, men began to talk about Eisenhower, marking him as someone to watch.

The payoff came almost immediately. After a short period as a staff officer in Georgia, Eisenhower went to Washington—General John J. Pershing, Chief of Staff of the U.S. Army, had requested his services. Pershing wanted someone to write a guide to the American World War I battlefields in France. The project was close to Pershing's heart and he wanted the best possible job done on it. Fox Connor told Pershing that Eisenhower was his man. So Eisenhower began to study World War I under the direct guidance of the general who had commanded the Americans in that war. It was an ideal assignment.

Eisenhower threw himself into the job as thoroughly as he had at Leavenworth. He had a six-month deadline. In that time he so thoroughly mastered the campaigns in France that Connor remarked, "Eisenhower knows more about our battles in Europe than anyone, including Pershing." Pershing was so pleased with the results that he wrote a glowing letter of praise, saying that Eisenhower "has shown superior ability not only in visualizing his work as a whole but in executing its many details in an efficient and timely manner. What he has done was accomplished only by the exercise of unusual intelligence and constant devotion to duty."

A month later, in September, 1927, Pershing assigned Eisenhower to the Army War College, the Army's top postgraduate school and one of the most advanced military schools in the world. At the War College students learned to think about the big problems in war—supply, movement of large bodies of troops, relations with allies, grand strategy. It was assumed that those who did well at the War College would become generals if the United States ever entered another conflict.

Eisenhower did well, as Pershing had expected, and after his graduation from the one-year course Pershing sent him off to France to study the battlefields at first hand, in the course of revising his guidebook. The Eisenhowers had a marvelous year abroad. They lived in Paris, where they visited all the famous sights. Along with John, now eight years old, they traveled throughout France. Eisenhower tried to learn French but found he had no talent for foreign languages; he did, however, become an expert on the French railroad and highway system, and on the French terrain in general. Mamie said that before they left, Ike knew every road in France. Years later, in the midst of World War II, he would make good use of the information he had memorized.

In 1929 Eisenhower returned to the States. Thirty-nine years old, he had been on special assignment, or at school, or on staff duty, for almost the whole of his career. He was still a major, with no real hope of rapid advancement in an army that was small in size and shrinking, at that. But he still hoped for a command of his own, a chance to get out into the field with troops and make some practical use of all the knowledge he had gained. Besides, only by getting a field assignment could he hope for promotion. But his talents as a staff officer were so obviously superior that nearly every general in the Army requested his services. Somewhat to Eisenhower's disgust he found himself stuck behind a desk once more. This time, however, it was one of the more important desks—he would be the assistant executive in the office of the U.S. Assistant Secretary of War.

chapter five

The Long and Dreary Thirties

Eisenhower spent the decade of the 1930s behind a series of desks, working as a staff officer without the responsibility of command. His reputation grew; he was known throughout the Army as a man who could write a clear report or a good speech, or prepare a careful study on a specific problem. He had no luck in getting field service with troops, but he did continue to broaden his outlook and deepen his education. At the time no one could have convinced Eisenhower that the constant staff duty was for his own good; that he was learning lessons that would be invaluable to him in 1944 as Supreme Commander, Allied Expeditionary Force; that although he did not have much experience in commanding a company of men he did know a great deal about logistics, the science of getting supplies from the factories to the front-line troops. As a desk officer working in Washington, Eisenhower learned to see war from the top, from the point of view of the high command. He could recognize the forest and not be distracted by the trees.

Eisenhower's big picture, however, did not include the nonmilitary world, though he lived in Washington during the Great Depression, when millions of Americans went without jobs and had nowhere to turn for aid and support. During this period the Government launched a series of extensive reform measures designed to restore the economy, coupled with relief programs to provide federal employment for the men out of work. It was a tremendously exciting time in Washington; emotions were aroused by the new politics to a degree seldom seen in the capital. Everyone seemed to take an extreme position on the new economic reforms and social programs, either denouncing them as dangerous or even evil, or praising them as the nation's salvation. Ike lived in the middle of this excitement (his brother Milton was deeply involved, serving as a high-ranking official in the Department of Agriculture), but the uproar had no effect on him. He still refused to discuss national problems or to make his feelings about politics known. The truth may be that he never devoted enough thought to politics to have an opinion. Certainly neither the Depression nor the reforms created to remedy it caused him to change his way of seeing domestic issues. He remained a simple soldier, somehow above or outside of politics.

Eisenhower's first Washington assignment in the Assistant Secretary of War's office was to pave the way for cooperation between industry and the War Department in the event of a future war. The United States had entered previous wars without any plans for mobilizing and using troops or for converting industry from peacetime to wartime production. In 1930, American industrial leaders were not expecting another war, and so no company in the country was making tanks or military airplanes or any of the thousands of items a massive army would require. Nothing had been done, for example, to prepare a company such as General Motors to switch from manufacturing Chevrolets to making Sherman tanks. Eisenhower, though only a major, was put in charge of planning for industrial conversion in the event of war—an astonishingly important job for a man not yet forty years old.

His job was frustrating, for most Americans were convinced that if war ever came, their country could make the necessary changes after it started—as the United States had done in the past. One man who disagreed was Bernard Baruch, who as Chairman of the War Industries Board in World War I had overseen industrial mobilization for that war. Eisenhower went to see Baruch, who warned him that the first great problem once war began would be competition between departments of government, with various departments placing conflicting orders with the same industrial firm. Without some direction from the top, a company with many orders for different goods would not know which to fill first.

When Eisenhower discussed these possible dangers with high officials in Washington, however, they scoffed at him, saying that cooperation between the Army and Navy would be enough to manage the problem. "All our experience has shown that this was foolishness," Eisenhower commented. "Even during a war against a common enemy, armies and navies of the same nation have often delighted in warring against each other for guns, men—and applause." Eisenhower did what he could to make realistic preparations for modern war, and eventually he wrote a brilliant plan for industrial mobilization. It cannot be said that his plan was actually used down to the last detail when World War II began, but it did provide the base on which others could build.

In the fall of 1930 General Douglas MacArthur became Chief of Staff of the Army; he immediately put Ike to work for him. The new Chief of Staff was a remarkable man. Supremely self-confident and amazingly self-centered, he acted as if the world revolved around him. He was accustomed to being fawned on and waited on, to having his own way, to being praised as a genius, and most of all, to being admired, even worshiped. MacArthur seemed to surround himself with "spit-lickers" —yes-men who considered it the highest honor just to be near the wondrous MacArthur. (One of MacArthur's aides, a three-star general, said that MacArthur was the greatest human being since Jesus Christ; another said he could be compared only to Napoleon.)

Strikingly handsome, MacArthur wore flashy, nonregulation uniforms that reminded observers more of a Latin American dictator or a comic-opera general than an officer of the United States Army. He came to his office around 11 A.M. and left after lunch, leaving all the work to his subordinates. He could not bear to be contradicted and he spoke of himself in the third person, much as European kings did. "So MacArthur told those congressmen," he would say, making it clear that once MacArthur had spoken, nothing more needed to be said.

MacArthur had indeed enjoyed a successful career. He

*A typically arrogant
General MacArthur.*

had made the highest marks any cadet had ever achieved
at West Point; he had commanded a division in France
in World War I, earning a chestful of medals; he had
been the Superintendent at West Point after the war and
was instrumental in bringing the West Point program up
to date, despite intense opposition from the old guard in
the Army. Now he was Chief of Staff.

Obviously MacArthur did not achieve such a record merely by posing—he was a man of great talent. Perhaps the most important of his talents was his ability to recognize capable men and get them to work for him. It only *seemed* that all his staff officers were yes-men; some were officers of marked ability. Chief among these was Eisenhower. These two men could not have been more different in personality and work habits; they never liked each other. But from the first time MacArthur met Eisenhower, he knew that he wanted Ike working for him. As early as 1931 MacArthur predicted that in the next war Eisenhower would go right to the top.

So from 1930 to 1939, Eisenhower served MacArthur. He never really enjoyed the duty, but as always he did the best he could. In 1965, when Eisenhower was asked about MacArthur, he said, "Oh, yes, I studied dramatics under him for ten years." In fact, he learned a lot more than dramatics, even if many of the lessons were negative. For example, Eisenhower was shocked at MacArthur's active participation in partisan politics, for Ike accepted the old Army tradition that soldiers should never discuss political issues, while MacArthur identified himself with the conservative right wing of the Republican Party and made it clear that he would welcome that party's nomination for the Presidency. But although MacArthur followed Army regulations and traditions only when it suited him, he was nonetheless an outstanding soldier with a great deal to teach.

MacArthur was not a good writer himself, so he had Eisenhower prepare his annual reports on the Army and write speeches and articles for him. MacArthur would give Eisenhower his ideas and the reasoning behind them, a procedure which forced Eisenhower to think in terms of the big picture. While other officers of his rank and age were dealing with problems involving a company, regiment, or post, Ike was working with the President's top assistants on problems of grand strategy and international relations. It was the ideal preparation for high command.

Being at the very pinnacle of the Army's organization chart had its rewards, but serving MacArthur could lead to embarrassment too. What Eisenhower later recalled as one of the worst moments of his life came in the summer of 1932, when MacArthur ordered him to go along on an expedition to force the Bonus Marchers out of Washington. The marchers were veterans of World War I, now unemployed at the depth of America's Great Depression. Out of work, with no prospects of getting jobs, unable to feed and shelter themselves, much less their families, twenty thousand veterans had thrown together a ramshackle camp across the Anacostia River just outside Washington, while others moved into abandoned buildings not far from the Capitol itself. They created a ragged appearance at best, and a possible health problem. Their aim was to put direct pressure on Congress to pay them an immediate bonus for their wartime services. Congress had already passed the bill to pay a bonus in 1945, but most of the veterans figured they would be long past any need for it by then. They announced that they would stay in Washington until the Government paid up.

The Bonus Marchers were the forerunners of the

numerous groups that have since used techniques of direct political pressure to force the Government to recognize their demands. To the conservative Republicans then in power, led by President Herbert Hoover, they seemed a menace to law and order, a direct challenge to the government, and possibly even heralded the beginning of a revolution. MacArthur assumed the Bonus Marchers were either agents or dupes of the Communist Party and they had to be taught a lesson. Most members of the Washington establishment agreed with him.

Eisenhower did not. He noted that the veterans had established military discipline in their camps, had gone to great lengths to make certain that none of their groups disturbed the peace of the capital, and generally conducted themselves with dignity and restraint. He thought they should be pitied and helped, not hounded or attacked. Though he was also politically conservative, Eisenhower saw no threat to the Republic from the Bonus Marchers and he thought they should be treated with respect and consideration.

But on July 28, 1932, Hoover ordered the Army to clear the Bonus Marchers out of Washington. MacArthur threw himself into the job with glee. Dressing in his flashiest uniform, he told Eisenhower to put on battle gear and prepare for action. Ike protested. He pointed out that it would be highly inappropriate for the Chief of Staff of the Army to go to the scene, especially since the Army would be moving against its own veterans. But MacArthur was convinced that a revolution was at hand and that it had to be stamped out immediately. He even ordered tanks brought up.

MacArthur used six hundred troops, with bayonets fixed, to drive the Bonus Marchers from their camp. He personally directed his soldiers' movements, with a red-faced Eisenhower at his side. Fortunately the veterans did not resist, aside from cursing at the troops (and of course at MacArthur), and no one was hurt, although the shacks in which the veterans lived were burned to the ground, along with all their possessions.

When it was over Eisenhower advised his boss to go home. He knew that newspaper reporters would surely want to interview the Chief of Staff, and his advice was to avoid them. Otherwise, Ike warned, the public would get the impression that MacArthur himself, not President Hoover, had made the decision to send American troops against starving, unarmed men. But MacArthur invited the reporters to interview him—and thereby brought down on his head the wrath of many who had sympathy for the veterans. Though they blamed MacArthur for the whole distasteful business, MacArthur did not mind, since he was also praised by conservatives who thought that the Chief of Staff had done just right. MacArthur, in truth, enjoyed being the center of controversy—a prospect that horrified Eisenhower.

Service with MacArthur was not always so exciting; most of the time Ike did routine work. He did it so well that he came to the attention of prominent men outside the Army. His reputation as a writer led a newspaper to offer him a job as military editor, at a salary of $20,000 a year, more than five times the amount he was making as an Army major. Ike gave the offer serious consideration. He seemed to be getting nowhere in the Army; his highest ambition was to become a colonel, but even that appeared to be impossible. His brothers—even Milton, the youngest—were far more successful than he was and were making considerably more money. But Ike enjoyed Army life, got satisfaction out of doing his job well, and still believed Fox Connor's prediction that sooner or later there would be another war. If war came, Ike wanted to make his contribution—not in a stateside training camp, but at the head of a combat outfit. That was his duty, what he had been trained for. He felt strongly that he owed it to the United States, if only as payment for his free education. He turned down the newspaper's offer.

In 1935 MacArthur's tour of duty as Chief of Staff ended. He accepted a position with the Commonwealth of the Philippines, a colony of the United States. The United States Congress had promised the Philippines independence in 1945, but meanwhile the government of the colony would be in local hands, under the supervision of the United States. Thus the Philippines were in somewhat the same relation to the United States as Canada was to England.

Before becoming independent the Philippines would need a defense force, so Manuel L. Quezon, President of the Commonwealth, hired MacArthur to train an army for him. MacArthur asked Eisenhower to join him in Manila, the Philippine capital, as military adviser. Eisenhower was surprised, for in his words MacArthur was "a mysterious, romantic figure far above the frailty of dependence on others," and it had never occurred to Ike that MacArthur *needed* anyone. Ike tried to get out of it by stressing the fact that he had been a staff officer for almost his entire career and deserved a line assignment with troops, not more desk duty. But MacArthur insisted, and as usual he got his way. In September, 1935, the Army put Eisenhower on detached duty, and he and Mamie and John sailed for the Philippines.

The MacArthur-Eisenhower team was the first of countless military-advisor groups the United States would send around the world and the only one to go out before World War II. Their object was to teach the Filipinos to use American arms, organize an army, and learn to defend their islands. Unlike later military advisor groups, however, MacArthur and Eisenhower had no arms to hand out and almost no money to work with. Eisenhower drew up a series of plans for the formation of a Filipino army, but Quezon sent each plan back, saying that he would have to reduce the size of the budget and thus of the proposed army. Eisenhower drafted so many plans that he could soon be heard muttering to himself, "They also serve who only draft and draft."

Lack of money led to an incident that put a permanent chill in Eisenhower's relationship with MacArthur. The General had decided that the people of Manila would like to see their budding army. He ordered Eisenhower to prepare plans to bring all the troops to the capital city, where they would camp on the outskirts of Manila so that the residents could visit with them. At the end of the week, MacArthur proposed to stage a parade in downtown Manila. Eisenhower protested that it was impossible to do such a thing on a limited budget—just bringing the troops to Manila would cost more than the Commonwealth could spare, never mind feeding them for a week and sending them back to their regular training camps. But MacArthur made it an order.

Eisenhower went to work on the project with a sinking heart. Soon enough Quezon heard of it and called him into his office. The President wanted to know what the hell was going on. Eisenhower was astonished, for he had assumed that MacArthur had cleared the project with the President of the Commonwealth. Quezon said he knew nothing about it. Eisenhower promised to check with MacArthur, but Quezon called MacArthur himself and blasted the General for throwing away such vast sums of money.

Eisenhower returned to his office, where he found a furious MacArthur. The General said he had never meant for Ike to proceed with preparations for the camp and parade, but only to investigate it quietly. He shouted orders to call the event off and never to make such a fool mistake again. Eisenhower was polite enough to refer to the whole thing as a misunderstanding, although he knew perfectly well that MacArthur had lied. His only comment was, "Never again were we on warm and cordial terms."

While he was in Manila, Eisenhower had another opportunity to leave the Army and become a rich man. The year was 1938: Adolf Hitler had taken power in Germany and had begun his anti-Semitic program, designed to kill or dispossess the Jews of Germany. Representatives of the sizable Jewish community in Manila contacted Ike and offered him a job traveling in China, Southeast Asia, and Indonesia to find a place where Jewish refugees from Germany could live without persecution. The pay would be $60,000 a year, plus expenses—more than ten times what Ike was making in the Army. In addition, the group promised to place the first five years' salary in a bank, a total of $300,000, which Eisenhower could claim if for any reason he decided he had to leave the job. Despite the obvious temptations, Eisenhower rejected the offer. With war clouds building in Europe, again he felt it was his duty to stay in the Army.

In September, 1939, Hitler's German army attacked Poland; England and France declared war on Germany; World War II was under way. Eisenhower immediately went to MacArthur. "General," he later recalled saying, "in my opinion the United States cannot remain out of this war for long. I want to go home as soon as possible. I want to participate in the preparatory work that I'm sure is going to be intense." MacArthur replied that Eisenhower was making a mistake—he should stick to his job in the Philippines, where as the number-two American officer he was far more important than he would be as a mere lieutenant colonel in an expanding American Army.

Eisenhower insisted that he be allowed to go back to the States. He reminded MacArthur that he had missed combat duty in World War I and that he was determined not to miss this crisis. MacArthur finally gave in.

Quezon, however, was even more insistent that Eisenhower stay in Manila. Partly because MacArthur never did any detailed work, partly because Eisenhower had never adopted an attitude of racial superiority in dealing with the Filipinos, but mainly because of the high level of Eisenhower's work, Quezon greatly admired him. The Philippine President wanted him to remain so badly that he shoved a blank contract in front of Ike and told him, "We'll tear up the old contract. I've already signed this one and it is filled in—except what you want as your emoluments for remaining. You will write that in."

"Mr. President," Eisenhower replied, "your offer is flattering. But no amount of money can make me change my mind. My entire life has been given to this one thing, my country and my profession. I want to be there if what I fear is going to come about actually happens."

Quezon finally accepted his decision. Then, at a farewell luncheon the President held at his palace, Quezon tried to show his appreciation of "all Ike had done for the Philippine nation" by giving him a $100,000 annuity policy. Ike refused. "But I want to see to it that Mamie is always provided for," Quezon insisted. Ike still said no—taking care of Mamie was his job. In the end Quezon had to content himself with giving Ike a medal, then making a speech. "Among all Ike's outstanding qualities," Quezon said, "the quality I regard most highly is this: whenever I asked Ike for an opinion I got an answer. It may not have been what I wanted to hear, it may have displeased me, but it was always a straightforward and honest answer."

The Eisenhower family returned to the States, arriving in San Francisco in late 1939. Their son John was ready now to begin college and he asked his father about West Point and an Army career. The discussion led Ike to explain his reasons for turning down so many attractive offers for civilian employment over the years, jobs which could have made him a rich man. Ike pointed out that he had been in the Army since 1911 and a commissioned officer for twenty-five years. During all that time he had been rated as superior by his senior officers. He had graduated at the head of the C&GS at Leavenworth; he had served directly under the Army's two most famous generals, Pershing and MacArthur. Yet he had just made the rank of lieutenant colonel and the most he could hope for was to become a full colonel before he retired. The Army's seniority system, which gave promotions only on the basis of time spent in the service, not ability, had held him back. If he could ever make colonel he might hope for faster promotions, since the seniority system applied only to ranks below colonel, but it would take a miracle for him to become a colonel. In short, John could not hope to become rich or famous in the Army.

John must have wondered why his father stayed in the Army at all. Ike explained that his Army experience had been "wonderfully interesting" and it had brought him into contact with "men of ability, honor, and a sense of high dedication to their country." Ike told his son he was happy in his work and had long ago refused to bother his head about promotion, for "the real satisfaction" was for a man to do the best he could. "My ambition in the Army was to make everybody I worked for regretful when I was ordered to other duty." Ike added that he had always been proud to be an officer in the United States Army.

At the heart of Ike's feelings there was a deep and profound patriotism. It was not a subject he discussed. For him, love of country was akin to his love for Mamie, something he felt at the very root of his being, and just as he would never dream of talking about Mamie in public, he was also reluctant to discuss his patriotism.

He once remarked that "professional soldiers do not like to get too sentimental about such things as the flag and love of country." He expressed some of his feelings about the privilege of serving his country, and John decided to go to West Point.

During the next year (while Hitler's armies overran Europe) Ike held a variety of assignments, all with troops, which delighted him. The Army was expanding rapidly and there were thousands of things that needed to be done to prepare, train, and equip all the new men. To add to his happiness, one morning in the fall of 1940 he got a letter from his old friend of the tank corps days, George Patton, who expected to get command of one of the new tank divisions the Army was organizing and wanted Ike for a regimental commander. Ike considered it too good to be true, but one never knew what wonders the War Department might perform, so he hopefully awaited developments. Then came a telegram from a friend in the War Department, asking him if he would object to returning to Washington to work on the staff.

Ike was dismayed. America was getting closer to entering the war every day, he was working with troops in the field, and he had Patton's promise of tank command in combat—but now they wanted him behind a Washington desk again. After considerable thought, he wrote to Washington, "In the first place, I want to make it clear that I am, and always have been, very serious in my belief that the individual's preferences and desires should have little, if any, weight in determining his assignment, when superior authority is making a decision in the matter." Then he said that if his own wishes were to be taken into consideration, he would rather do anything than return to Washington. The letter worked—the request for his services was dropped.

Ike might as well have taken the Washington job, for in a short time he found himself back behind a desk anyway, this time as Chief of Staff to the Third Army in San Antonio. On their twenty-fifth wedding anniversary, he and Mamie arrived in the city where they had met. Ike was soon gone, however, on maneuvers in Louisiana, where he did so well that he was promoted to colonel and then, incredibly, to wear the stars of a brigadier general. Both ranks were only temporary—that is, when the Army went back to its normal size after the war, Ike would drop back to lieutenant colonel—but the promotions were so far above his expectations that he could hardly believe his good fortune. "Things are moving so rapidly these days," he wrote a friend, "that I get almost dizzy trying to keep up with the parade. One thing is certain—when they get clear down to my place on the list, they are passing out stars with considerable abandon."

A few days later, December 7, 1941, a Sunday, Eisenhower spent the morning working in his office. He had been pushing himself hard for months, putting in fifteen or more hours a day, and he was tired. He decided to go home to take a nap. Telling Mamie not to wake him for any reason, he flung himself down on the bed and fell into a deep sleep.

An hour later his aide called and insisted that Mamie wake the General. The Japanese had attacked Pearl Harbor and the Philippines. America had entered World War II.

The evil genius of the 20th century, his name was probably Schicklgrüber, but he was known as Adolf Hitler. House painter turned dictator, leader of the Nazi Party, and Chancellor of Germany from 1933 until his death in Berlin in 1945, he exterminated millions of people in his attempt to rid the world of Jews, Poles, Gypsies, Communists—anyone he personally labeled inferior.

chapter six

Marshall Grooms Ike for High Command

On December 14, 1941, Eisenhower walked into the office of the Army Chief of Staff, General George C. Marshall. Ike had just arrived in Washington, in accordance with rush orders from the War Department, and had not even unpacked his suitcase, much less found a place to stay. All of Washington was in a hubbub, for the city was the center of the American war effort and, since Pearl Harbor a week earlier, the country had been involved in frantic efforts to prepare for a war that was already under way. Beyond the hectic activity, the nation's mood was one of shocked outrage at the sneak attack and deep shame over the resounding defeat the Japanese had inflicted on American outposts in Hawaii and the Philippines. Inside the War Department, however, Eisenhower found another mood—one of grim determination. The officers he met in the halls were setting about their tasks in a workmanlike manner, determined to build an army that would teach the Japanese a lesson.

George Marshall had created the businesslike atmosphere. Eisenhower had talked with Marshall only twice, and then briefly, but he knew the Chief of Staff was a no-nonsense commander who insisted on getting things done. Ike realized that his orders to report to Washington had come directly from Marshall, but he had no idea what the General wanted him to do. So as he entered the Chief of Staff's office he was curious, a little afraid, but most of all, anxious to get to work.

Marshall briefly acknowledged Eisenhower's greeting, then outlined the military situation in the Far East. America had lost all of its Pacific fleet at Pearl Harbor except for the aircraft carriers, while the best part of the Air Force had been destroyed in the Philippines. The Japanese had landed on Luzon and were threatening Manila. They were on the verge of taking the two major British bases in the Pacific—Hong Kong and Singapore. Japanese ships ruled the seas of the Far East, while their airplanes controlled the skies. The Philippines were surrounded, cut off from the rest of the world.

Suddenly Marshall looked straight at Eisenhower and quietly demanded, "What should be our general line of action?"

Eisenhower was startled. He had just arrived, knew little more than what he had read in the newspapers and what Marshall had just told him, did not know what war plans had been made by the high command, and had no staff to help him prepare an answer. But he sensed that his entire career would depend on his answer. If he did well, Marshall would give him further important assignments and even heavier responsibilities; if he did poorly, Marshall would ship him out to a training camp at once, for Marshall had no time to waste. The Chief of Staff wanted to know who could do the job for him, and who could not, and he wanted to know it *now*. After a second or two of hesitation, Eisenhower said, "Give me a few hours." Marshall nodded and turned his attention to other pressing business.

Eisenhower went to a desk in the War Plans Division of the War Department, stuck a single sheet of yellow paper into an old typewriter, and began to peck out his answer to Marshall's question. He had been trained at Leavenworth to deal with such strategic problems, but this time it was the real thing, not an academic exercise. He typed "Steps To Be Taken" at the top of the page, then began writing. The first requirement was to "build up in Australia a base of operations from which supplies and personnel can be moved into the Philippines. Speed is essential." Australia had numerous advantages. If it became the major American base in the Pacific it would be fairly safe, since it was so far south of Japan, and it had good harbors, British Commonwealth connections, and English-speaking people. All prewar plans had called for using the Philippines as a base of operations, but from Marshall's description and from what he himself knew about the state of Philippine defenses, Eisenhower realized that the Islands could not be held. He was the first American officer to face up to this fact and to suggest that the War Department turn its attention to Australia. In the rest of his answer, Eisenhower outlined the methods by which the buildup of American forces in Australia could begin.

Eisenhower took his paper to Marshall, saying as he handed it to the Chief that it would be impossible to save the Philippines, but the United States had to do all it could, because "the people of [Asia] will be watching us. They may excuse failure but they will not excuse abandonment." Marshall said softly, "I agree with you." Then he added, "Do your best to save them." Ike had passed the test. Marshall put him in charge of the Philippines and Far Eastern Section of the War Plans Division.

Then Marshall leaned forward (Eisenhower recalled years later that the Chief had "an eye that seemed to me awfully cold") and declared, "Eisenhower, the Department is filled with able men who analyze their problems well but feel compelled always to bring them to me for final solution. I must have assistants who will solve their own problems and tell me later what they have done."

George Marshall's back had no bend to it. He carried himself with great dignity. His movements were deliberate, his shoulders square, his dress immaculate. His face looked as if it were chiseled out of stone. He had a determined jaw, a firm mouth, and deep-set, penetrating eyes. He commanded attention wherever he went, and he scared hell out of most people.

He had few intimate friends—no one called him George, not even President Franklin Roosevelt. When he relaxed he did it alone, watching movies or puttering in his garden. His sense of humor was limited and he kept a tight grip on his emotions. To those who could do the work and who shared his sense of duty, Marshall was intensely loyal. But he did his best to keep from showing his feelings of affection, perhaps out of fear of appearing weak. For example, hardly anyone could resist Ike's boyish grin or his catchy nickname, but although he worked for Marshall for four years, in all that time Marshall never called him anything but "Eisenhower." (At the victory parade in New York City at the end of the war Marshall slipped and called him "Ike"; to make up for it, he used "Eisenhower" five times in his next sentence.)

Once when Eisenhower was in Marshall's office, a few weeks after the war began, Marshall leaned forward to explain his attitude toward promotion. "The men who are going to get the promotions in this war are the commanders in the field, not the staff officers who clutter up all of the administrative machinery in the War Department. . . . The field commanders carry the responsibility and I'm going to see to it that they're properly rewarded so far as promotion can provide a reward.

"Take your case," he continued, looking at Eisenhower. "I know that you were recommended by one general for division command and by another for corps command. That's all very well . . . but you are going to stay right here and fill your position, and that's that!" Preparing to turn to other business, Marshall muttered, "While this may seem a sacrifice to you, that's the way it must be."

Eisenhower's sense of duty was as sharp as Marshall's and he had already reached a rank he had not thought possible. He resented being singled out for the lecture, especially since he had already missed command in the field in World War I. "General, I'm interested in what you say," he blurted out, "but I want you to know that I

George C. Marshall, perhaps the finest soldier America has ever produced and a genius at planning and organizing, was the brains behind the whole Allied effort in World War II.

don't give a damn about your promotion plans as far as I'm concerned. I came into this office . . . and I am trying to do my duty. I expect to do so as long as you want me here. If that locks me to a desk for the rest of the war, so be it!"

Pushing back his chair, Eisenhower strode toward the door. It was a big office and a long walk. By the time he reached the door his anger had gone. He turned, looked at Marshall, and grinned. As he closed the door he thought he saw a tiny smile at the corners of Marshall's mouth.

Two weeks later Marshall recommended Eisenhower for promotion to major general. The Chief explained that Ike was not just a staff officer, but his operations officer, a sort of subordinate commander. On March 27, 1942, Eisenhower got his second star.

There was a father-son quality to the Marshall-Eisenhower relationship. They were not "pals," but they had deep respect for each other. To the Chief's face, and in discussing him with others, Eisenhower always called him "General." There was never any doubt that Marshall was the superior, but the General was terribly proud of Ike and gave him unlimited support and guidance.

Marshall was a genius—in Eisenhower's view, one of the great Americans of all time. He was the head of the Army's war effort and, next to President Roosevelt, the most powerful man in Washington. Over the next four years he would set the broad policies for Allied war operations, create the military organization, and make the major strategic decisions. In these areas Eisenhower would follow, for he was the perfect man to translate Marshall's views and thoughts into practice. Together, they made an outstanding team.

The partnership began on December 14, 1941, and did not end until the war was over. From the first, therefore, Eisenhower was dealing with the really tough problems, seeing the war from the top. He carried an immense responsibility, but he carried it easily. And he never once let Marshall down.

For America, World War II was a global conflict. In the Pacific the enemy was Japan. Japan was ruled by its military and was determined to expand its frontiers. The Japanese aimed to boot the white man out of Asia and take control of it for themselves; this meant driving the Americans out of the Philippines, the French out of Indochina, the British out of Hong Kong, Malaya, Burma, and India, and the Dutch out of Indonesia. Under ordinary circumstances the Japanese could not have hoped to deal with a combination of such powerful enemies, but the Dutch and French had already been defeated by the Germans in 1940, and though Britain was still unconquered it was preoccupied with the struggle against Germany.

The Americans were not particularly anxious to fight for the British, Dutch, and French empires in Asia, and they had already decided to give the Philippines its independence. But they could not allow the Japanese to take over the whole area by force because they would keep non-Asians, including Americans, out altogether, denying them the right to sell goods in Asia, or to extract raw materials. Japan would keep the markets and the materials for itself, thereby becoming the major power in the Pacific. Fighting Japan, the United States became, in effect, the defender of white men's rule in Asia.

Japan's allies in Europe were Germany and Italy; both declared war on the United States three days after Pearl Harbor. Italy was ruled by the Fascist Party under

Benito Mussolini, an inefficient dictator who dreamed of restoring the glorious empire of ancient Rome. But Italy had little industry, its Army was badly trained and poorly equipped, and its leadership was woefully inadequate. Italy had tried to invade Greece in 1941, failed, and had to be rescued by Hitler. In North Africa the Italians attempted to drive the British out of Egypt, in order to take control of the Suez Canal and cut Britain's lifeline to India, but the British Army had soundly defeated the Italians. Again Hitler had come to the rescue, sending Field Marshal Erwin Rommel and the Afrika Korps of tanks to the desert and thereby restoring the balance. Italy was the weakest of the three Axis partners by far.

Germany was the strongest member of the Axis alliance. It had more heavy industry than any country in the world except America, and German industry had been converted to wartime production since the mid-thirties. Tanks were rolling off German assembly lines while the Americans were still producing passenger cars. Germany had a fanatic but highly intelligent and ruthless leadership in Hitler and his generals. Its people were the best-educated in Europe, possibly in the world. The German Army was magnificently equipped and had professional leaders with a reputation for being the finest anywhere. Hitler aimed at the conquest of Europe, and in two years, from 1939 to 1941, his armies had overrun Poland, Norway, Belgium, Holland, France, Greece, Yugoslavia, and the European part of Russia. Rumania, Hungary, and Italy were allies of the Germans, while Spain was a friendly neutral. In short, by 1941 the Germans had taken control of the whole of Europe, something not even Napoleon had been able to accomplish.

Germany was ruled by the Nazi Party under the leadership of Adolf Hitler. Hitler was perhaps the most thoroughly evil statesman in modern history. He was able to rise to power for a number of reasons, but chief among them was his use of anti-Semitism. He blamed the Jews for Germany's loss of World War I, for the Depression of the thirties, indeed for all Germany's ills. Once in power he began a campaign to destroy all the Jews of Europe. After overrunning Europe, he set up concentration camps throughout the conquered territory, where his Nazi henchmen put Jews into gas chambers, then burned the bodies. By the end of the war he had supervised the slaughter of nearly six million Jews. The Nazis were not only anti-Semitic. Hitler believed that the Germans constituted a master race which was destined to rule the world. He regarded Poles, Negroes, Russians, Gypsies—anyone who was not German—as inferior scum who should either get out of the way or serve as slaves for the "master race." His ideas about race in general, and especially about the natural superiority of Germanic peoples, had no basis in scientific fact, but nevertheless he convinced millions of Germans that they were giants in a world of midgets.

As a military leader Hitler was a great risk-taker, willing to gamble everything on one roll of the dice. He had shown this in a number of situations, but never more clearly than when he decided to invade giant Russia in June, 1941. His generals had opposed the invasion, arguing that first Hitler must either conquer or make peace with Britain, so that Germany would not have to fight on two fronts. Hitler, however, had no fear of taking on both Russia and Britain at once and ordered the invasion to begin. The Germans were successful; they captured over two million Russian prisoners in the first three months of the campaign, and almost took Moscow itself. When America entered the war Germany was at the very gates of the Russian capital and most observers thought that Russia would soon be forced to surrender.

There were some people in the United States who thought that a German victory over Russia might not be so bad. They argued that there was little difference between Hitler's fascist Germany and Joseph Stalin's communist Russia. In fact, most conservatives tended to be more afraid of Stalin than of Hitler, and at this time the American public as a whole was generally afraid of Communism. In early 1942 Senator Harry Truman suggested that the best outcome would be for Germany and Russia to beat each other to death. Senior Army officers were saying that the Russians were doomed anyway, so the Americans should plan to carry on the war without them and should not waste any resources trying to help the Russian Red Army.

One of Eisenhower's major contributions to the war was to put an immediate stop to such talk. Like most Americans, Eisenhower was anti-Communist, although— again like most of his countrymen—he had only a vague idea of what Communism meant. But he also realized that the immediate danger was Germany. It was, after all, the Germans who meant to conquer all of Europe, not the Russians; it was the Germans who had secretly attacked Russia, not vice versa. And in any case the Germans could never be defeated without the help of the Red Army. Eisenhower insisted from the first that it would be "the greatest blunder in all military history" to allow Russia's army, an army of eight million men, to fall without trying to save it.

Eisenhower made this clear in a late February memorandum. The fundamental military fact of World War II, he recognized, was the Russo-German war. Here was where the major forces were engaged, where the greatest killing was done, where the stakes were the highest. Whoever won on the German-Russian front would win the war. The issue of the future of Europe would be decided on the banks of the Volga River, where Germany had most of her troops engaged—not in the South China Sea or in the Central Pacific or in the Egyptian desert. Eisenhower gave Marshall a list of the main American objectives; in it he insisted on the difference between those operations which were "*necessary* to the ultimate defeat of the Axis Powers" and those which "are merely *desirable*." The necessary included only two items—keep both Britain *and* Russia in the war. Everything else was merely desirable.

For the Americans, unlike their allies in London and Moscow, the issue was not to defend themselves against direct attack on the homeland but, rather, to keep the world balance of power. If Germany and its junior partner, Italy, came to control all of Europe, while Japan took Asia, America would suffer a major economic blow, since it would be unable to trade with the rest of the world. And eventually the United States itself might be attacked by the Axis.

For Marshall and Eisenhower at the beginning of 1942

the first strategic problems were to get together with the British in order to coordinate their activities, stop the Axis advance around the world, build an American Army, Navy, and Air Force, and then start the counter-offensive. The last problem promised to be the hardest because the Allies could attack the Axis Powers *only* through a seaborne invasion, and they first had to get troops ashore, whether it be in occupied Europe or on the Pacific islands. To get ashore they would need to work out invasion techniques, build landing craft, and solve all sorts of supply problems. There were no past lessons they could draw on for help, since modern military history gave no examples of successful sea-to-shore invasions. Many military experts considered it impossible to land men on a hostile shore against any kind of determined opposition. But unless the Allies could figure out a way to do just this, they might as well give up at once and save time, money, and lives.

It was equally important to decide *where* to make the major effort in a two-front war. Many Americans, furious at the Japanese attack on Pearl Harbor, wanted to turn the whole American force against Japan. The British, living under Hitler's guns, were more concerned about the war in Europe. Early in 1942 the British Chiefs of Staff (BCOS) came to Washington to discuss the problem with the American Joint Chiefs of Staff (JCS). Marshall asked Eisenhower for his opinion, and Ike prepared another of his long reports. In this one he discussed the advantages of each approach. He concluded that in his view Europe was much more important than Asia and Germany much stronger than Japan; therefore the major effort ought to be made in Europe against Hitler. Eisenhower argued that if Germany were beaten, Japan could never hold out alone, but if Japan were beaten, Germany might well win the war anyway. Marshall agreed, and so of course did the British. At their first wartime meeting, therefore, the two countries made their most significant agreement—to concentrate against the Germans. They would turn the offensive power of the Alliance against Hitler, fighting a defensive war in the Pacific until Germany surrendered.

Another crucial agreement came out of that first British-American meeting. Never before in history had two allies fought side by side on a single front. National jealousies were such that when England and France had combined against Germany in World War I, neither nation would allow a general from the other to command its troops. In effect the French had fought one war, the British another. Marshall was determined to avoid such a waste of effort in World War II, and he used arguments prepared by Eisenhower to convince the British to make war under the direction of a single commander. The BCOS was opposed at first, since it did not like the idea of putting a British admiral under the command of an American general, but eventually Marshall and Eisenhower convinced them, and the principle of unity of command was established.

Unity of command meant that the Allies would divide the world into several spheres or theaters, then assign a Supreme Commander for each theater. One man would be in charge in Europe, one in the Southwest Pacific, one in the Central Pacific, and one in South Asia. It was an ambitious undertaking, never tried before, but Marshall and Eisenhower insisted that it would work. For overall, worldwide command, the two powers then created the Combined Chiefs of Staff (CCS), composed of the BCOS and the JCS. The CCS would give orders to the various Supreme Commanders; in turn the CCS received its orders from the two heads of government, British Prime Minister Winston Churchill and President Roosevelt.

In their first meeting, then, the Americans and British agreed on a strategy of tackling Europe first, and on a command for carrying out the war. They thereby created the firmest alliance in history. Eventually Eisenhower became the symbol and the most famous leader of that alliance, so it was fitting that he had played a key role in setting it up.

Agreement on exactly where to begin the attack did not come so easily. Marshall and Eisenhower wanted to get right down to business, so they proposed that the Allies invade German-occupied France in the fall of 1942. Ike argued that such an invasion was the only way the Allies could help beleagured Russia, because it would pull German troops from the Russian front to defend their control of France. Keeping Russia in the war was the key to victory. The British did not want to see the Russian Red Army defeated either, but they were not so sure that an invasion of France was the way to help. In the British view the invasion could not possibly succeed—America had just begun to mobilize for war and had few tanks and even fewer landing craft, while Britain was worn down from two and a half years of fighting. An unsuccessful invasion would do the Russians no good and do the Al-

Ike and Marshall share a rare moment of relaxation. Marshall was something of a father figure for Ike, grooming him for high command and making sure Ike succeeded there.

lies a lot of harm. The British, therefore, proposed that in the fall of 1942 the Allies invade an easier target— either Axis-controlled North Africa or Norway.

The CCS spent much of the early part of 1942 arguing about whether or not to attack France or North Africa the next fall; Eisenhower was at Marshall's side during the entire discussion. The two factions did agree to begin building up an American force in Britain in the meantime, but that did not settle the dispute, for once the buildup was complete the force could be used against either target. Still, it was a beginning.

In early June, 1942, the BCOS came to America for another conference with the JCS. This time they were able to reach agreement. The American buildup in England would continue; meanwhile the two allies would prepare a "suicide" operation for the fall of 1942. Code-named SLEDGEHAMMER, this was designed to force an early Allied landing on the French coast. SLEDGEHAMMER was an emergency operation without hope of real success; it would actually go ahead only if the Red Army appeared to be on the verge of surrender. The British were sure SLEDGEHAMMER could not possibly work, and even the Americans had their doubts, but it was the least the Allies could do to help if the situation around Moscow became desperate. Otherwise, if Germany defeated Russia, it could turn its whole force against Britain and America.

If the Russians were able to hold on, there would be no SLEDGEHAMMER. In that event, the CCS agreed to launch the main invasion of Europe in the spring of 1943 (code name, ROUNDUP). By then America's factories should have turned out enough landing craft, tanks, airplanes, and other implements of war to make the invasion force powerful enough to succeed.

With the basic strategy settled, it was time to put someone in command. Marshall had Eisenhower write a draft directive for the American commander in Britain to take SLEDGEHAMMER and ROUNDUP into account, and to create the U.S. Army's European Theater of Operations (ETO). Eisenhower did so, then handed the draft to Marshall, asking the Chief to read it carefully because it could be an important document in the further waging of the war. Marshall replied, "I certainly do want to read it. You may be the man who executes it. If that's the case, when can you leave?"

Eisenhower was thunderstruck. He had resigned himself to spending the war in Washington and had no idea that Marshall had been grooming him for high command. Marshall was finally giving him service with troops—the most important field command in the Allied military machine, at that. As a bonus he would be carrying out strategy he had helped to create.

Eisenhower was given command of ETO because he had fulfilled all of Marshall's expectations and met all his tests. But Eisenhower's achievements to date had been as a desk officer, usually serving under strong-willed superiors. The men under whom he had worked, including MacArthur, had thought he would be successful as an independent commander, but that was only prediction. No one really knew how he would react when commanding on his own, away from the daily influence of a decisive superior. Eisenhower still had to meet that test.

chapter seven
Lighting the TORCH

On June 24, 1942, Eisenhower arrived in England. He would not see his family again until 1944. He immediately set to work gathering a staff to assist him with his duties as head of the European Theater of Operations and as commander of SLEDGEHAMMER. Ike once commented that he had been a staff officer longer than anyone else in the Army, so he ought to know how to put together a good staff. His emphasis was on teamwork. Drawing on his football coaching methods, he insisted that the staff provide coordinated effort rather than flashy individual performances. He moved ETO headquarters out of London to the English countryside in order to get the staff living together "like a football team" and so that the officers could "think war, plan war, and execute war twenty-four hours a day, or at least all of our waking hours."

"War has become so comprehensive and so complicated that teamwork seems to me to be the essence of all success," Eisenhower told his assembled staff officers. Because he thought that "no successful staff can have any personal enmities existing in it," he insisted on having a happy family. "I want to see a big crowd of friends around here," he said. Before the war was over, Eisenhower would have a staff of over two thousand officers and enlisted men, but he never lost sight of the goals he set in mid-1942, and much of his success in the war was due to the outstanding staff he put together and directed. It was far from being the most exciting part of his job, but it was the most important; without a staff to provide information, ideas, plans, and supplies, he would have been helpless. The days when a general like Napoleon or U. S. Grant could direct an entire war by himself were gone; war had become much too complicated for that.

Eisenhower felt the need of a strong Chief of Staff, someone who could direct the day-to-day activities in his office. He had in mind General Walter Bedell Smith, a truly outstanding soldier who was working for Marshall. Marshall did not want to lose Smith's services, but Ike insisted, and Marshall finally gave in. Smith spent the remainder of the war at Eisenhower's side; he was the indispensable man. Smith "is a natural-born chief of staff and really takes charge of things in a big way," Ike said shortly after Smith arrived. "I wish I had a dozen like him. If I did, I would simply buy a fishing rod and write home every week about my wonderful accomplishments in winning the war."

A task as important as building a staff was training the American GI's coming into England. Eisenhower

Walter Bedell Smith was Ike's right-hand man. Ike called him "a natural-born chief of staff."

spent much of his time visiting the troops, checking on their progress, showing them how to use new weapons, and insisting that they get out into the field for exercises and war games. Most necessary of all, he felt, was good discipline. If the Army had it, it would convince the British "that we are here not as muddling amateurs but as earnest, competent soldiers who know what we are about."

Eisenhower was also concerned with the quality of his field commanders. He explained his feelings on the subject to a friend: "This is a long tough road we have to travel. . . . The men that can do things are going to be sought out just as surely as the sun rises in the morning. Fake reputations, habits of glib and clever speech, and glittering surface performance are going to be discovered and kicked overboard." For an officer to make it in this war, he had to be a leader with "inexhaustible nervous energy . . . and iron-clad determination to face discouragement, risk, and increasing work without flinching." He would also need imagination—Ike confessed that he was "continuously astounded by the utter lack of imaginative thinking among so many of our people that have reputations for being really good officers." Finally, an officer had to be able to forget himself and his personal fortunes.

Eisenhower needed "inexhaustible nervous energy" himself, for while he was putting together the staff, overseeing the training of troops, and selecting field commanders, he was also involved in one of the great strategic arguments of the war. The British had gone sour on SLEDGEHAMMER. The most notable critic was the Prime Minister, Winston Churchill. A short fat man with pudgy jowls and a look that seemed childishly innocent, Churchill was a volcano of activity. Unlike Roosevelt, who left the details of waging the war to the JCS, Churchill considered war far too important to be left to the generals— he meddled in everything. He was, indeed, almost a part of the BCOS, attending most of its meetings and second-guessing his high-ranking military at every turn. Churchill considered himself a military genius, which was far from the truth, but as Prime Minister he was able to insert his views into every operation of the war.

SLEDGEHAMMER, in Churchill's opinion, was hopeless. The Americans could not possibly build enough tanks and landing craft, or train enough men, to invade Europe in 1942, and the British were so thoroughly engaged against Nazi Field Marshal Erwin Rommel's forces in Egypt that they could not handle the operation alone. Besides, Churchill was not at all anxious to fight the German Army so close to its homeland, on the plains of Northwest Europe. He had fought in the trenches on the Western Front in World War I, where so much British blood had been needlessly spilled, and he was determined that in this war there would be no more bloodbaths.

In Churchill's view the way to win the war was to encircle the Germans ("closing the ring," he called it) by attacking them around the edges of the territory they had conquered; the best places to attack were small German outposts, such as those in Norway and North Africa. Meanwhile the Russians could continue to engage the bulk of the German Army. Churchill felt the Western Allies should wait until the German Army had exhausted itself in Russia, and only then invade Europe. The major advantage of such an approach would be fewer British casualties.

Eisenhower and Marshall disagreed. The Americans had not tasted defeat at the hands of the Germans, as had the British; they had not been kicked off the Continent by Hitler's troops, as the British had in 1940 at Dun-

Winston Churchill, with his great bulk and unconquerable will, came to symbolize the Allied cause. The Prime Minister's cigar was as much his trademark as his two-finger "V for Victory" salute.

kirk. The Americans wanted to get down to business, which meant coming to grips with the main German force in France as soon as possible. Eisenhower and Marshall wanted to defeat Hitler quickly so that the United States could turn its power against Japan.

The strategic issue was this: Should the Allies take grave risks in order to invade France as soon as possible, or should they wait until their strength grew while German power was reduced by the Russians?

Eisenhower feared a diversion—if the Allies hit a lesser target, such as Norway or North Africa, in 1942, they would be tied down and unable to launch the main invasion of Europe, ROUNDUP, in 1943. In other words, mounting an offensive in 1942 would mean postponing the invasion of France to 1944. Churchill insisted that Eisenhower was wrong—the Prime Minister said that the Allies could mount a 1942 offensive and still have enough force left for ROUNDUP.

As the American Commander in England, Eisenhower bore the brunt of the argument with Churchill. It took a lot out of Ike, partly because Churchill was remarkably persistent, partly because of the Prime Minister's habits. Churchill ordinarily woke during midafternoon and began his working day after dinner, continuing until four or five in the morning. He frequently called Ike on the telephone at midnight or even later, asking him to come to his office for a conference. Eisenhower took the strain well, mainly because of his great fund of patience but also because of his great love for Churchill. Despite their different views, the two men got along famously and spent as much time together as they could.

Through most of July, 1942, Eisenhower and Churchill argued. Toward the end of the month Marshall and the other members of the JCS came to London for a CCS meeting. Neither side would give in. Churchill finally went over the heads of the military men and convinced Roosevelt that the most important thing was for American troops to attack the Germans somewhere in 1942, for if they waited for ROUNDUP it would be a full two years after Pearl Harbor before America began its first offensive. Roosevelt ordered Marshall to work something out with the British that would put American troops into action in 1942. This was one of the few times in the war that the President interfered in a military decision. Marshall decided that North Africa was a better target than Norway, so on July 22 he informed the British that the Americans agreed to an invasion of Algeria.

Eisenhower was depressed by the decision. At breakfast on July 23 he muttered to an aide, "I hardly know where to start today." He thought that July 22 "could well go down as the blackest day in history," for he was sure that the decision would delay the end of the war by at least a year. He had spent six months working on plans to invade France in late 1942 or early 1943; now, he felt that invasion could not come before 1944—and events proved him correct. But he was also a soldier who did what he was ordered to do by the President, so despite his mood he gathered his staff together and they "settled down to assemble pieces of the wreckage of their plans." SLEDGEHAMMER and ROUNDUP were in the ash can. It was time to start all over.

The new operation was given the code name TORCH; the CCS made Eisenhower its commander. TORCH called for a British-American force to land in French-controlled Algeria and Morocco, then drive east to Tunisia, where it would join with the British Eighth Army, under General Bernard L. Montgomery, coming west from Egypt. Between them, Eisenhower's and Montgomery's forces would crush the Italians and Rommel's Afrika Korps, clear North Africa of the enemy, and give the Allies a firm striking position on Europe's southern flank.

There were all sorts of complications to TORCH. Since there had never been a successful sea-to-shore invasion in recent military history, Eisenhower had no lessons to draw on—he could only do his best and then hope luck would see him through. He would be commanding navies and air forces as well as ground troops—again a unique situation. And he would be giving orders to the British units as well as to the Americans—another unprecedented task. The problems were enormous. In the middle of handling them, Eisenhower confessed in a letter to Patton (who was given command of the American unit attacking the African West Coast), "I feel like the lady in the circus that has to ride three horses with no very good idea of exactly where any one of the three is going to go."

Ike remained sure of one thing—if the British and Americans did not get along with each other the invasion would fail and the Allies could lose the entire war. The key to success was cooperation and if it could not be achieved in the first joint operation, it might never be. He became, in his own words, a fanatic on the subject of British-American cooperation. Ike set an example by integrating his own staff, with both British and American officers working directly under him. And he flushed out any American officer he found guilty of anti-British feelings.

Once, hearing of an American general who, when drinking, had boasted that the Americans would show the British how to fight, Ike went white with rage. He told an aide to arrange for the general to report the next morning. As the aide left the room, Eisenhower growled "I'll make the son of a bitch swim back to America." The next day he sent the officer home—by boat. Some time later, Eisenhower learned of a fracas between an American and a British officer on his staff. He investigated, decided that the American was at fault, ordered him reduced in rank, and sent him back to the States. The British officer involved called on Ike to protest. "He only called me the son of a bitch, sir, and all of us have now learnt that this is a colloquial expression which is sometimes used almost as a term of endearment." To which Eisenhower replied, "I am informed that he called you a *British* son of a bitch. That is quite different. My ruling stands."

Eisenhower had a different set of problems with the French. In 1940 France had surrendered to the Nazis. The Germans had taken control of Paris and had occupied northern France, but they allowed the French to retain control of the southern half of the country, to maintain a government at Vichy, and to hold on to their colonies, including Morocco and Algeria in northwest Africa. The Vichy government became a Nazi satellite, though it called itself neutral. Vichy announced that it would defend its colonies against all comers. The Allies were planning to invade France's African colonies in order to get at the Axis stronghold in Tunisia, but they did not want to make war on France itself. Eisenhower hoped that the French officials in northwest Africa would break from the Vichy government and join in the Allies' war against Hitler. To get them to do so, however, he needed a French leader who would be willing to go against the Vichy government's orders.

One candidate for pro-Allied leadership of the French was Charles de Gaulle, a prominent general and a hero to the civilians in occupied France. De Gaulle had refused to obey his government's order to surrender and had gone instead to England, where he set up headquarters in London. De Gaulle rallied a number of Frenchmen to his side, disavowed the Vichy government, and was instrumental in the French Resistance movement; he called his headquarters Free France and insisted that only he represented the true France. Churchill liked and supported de Gaulle, but Roosevelt did not (primarily for personal reasons) and neither did the French officers in Vichy-controlled Algeria—after all, de Gaulle had branded them as traitors. So a combination of factors ruled de Gaulle out of consideration as Eisenhower searched for a French ally in North Africa.

Ike turned to General Henri Giraud, a one-legged French officer who had escaped from a German prison camp. He hoped that Giraud would be able to bring the French colonial army to the Allied side, so that the Allies would not have to fight for Algeria. If the French cooperated, Eisenhower could march his troops directly east, toward the true objective, Tunisia. If Giraud failed,

The Allies hoped General Giraud would bring French North Africa into the war on their side.

Eisenhower's troops would have to fight through the Algerian French in order to get at the Axis.

A major difficulty was Eisenhower's lack of political knowledge and sophistication. He simply did not understand the situation in France. The Vichy government was filled with conservative, right-wing leaders who thought Hitler had the right idea about how to run a country. Representing the old guard in the Army, the ranking members of the Catholic Church, and the great industrialists and landowners of France, Vichy was not really neutral, as it claimed, but a fascist government in collaboration with the Nazis. Eisenhower ignored this; remaining convinced that *all* Frenchmen were eager to be free of the Nazis, he paid no attention to Vichy's pro-Nazi views. That neglect would give him serious trouble.

On November 7, 1942, Eisenhower flew to Gibraltar, where he set up his command post headquarters. The next day the invasion of Africa began. Giraud issued orders to the French Army not to resist the Allied landings at Casablanca, Oran, and Algiers, but the French soldiers fired on the Allies anyway, because Giraud, in fact, had no position in the French Army and no right to give orders to anyone.

After two days of heavy fighting between the French and the Allies, Eisenhower's representatives in Algeria were able to get the commander in chief of Vichy's armed forces, Admiral Jean-François Darlan, to order a cease-fire. Darlan cooperated because Eisenhower's aides had promised him leadership of the government in the French colonies. Since Darlan was their legitimate superior, the French officers obeyed him and ordered their men to stop fighting. Eisenhower went to Algiers the next day to make the deal official with Darlan. Now, he thought, he could finally get down to the business of attacking the Germans in Tunisia.

He was wrong. The Darlan Deal set off a raging political battle in England and America. Darlan was a fascist. He had helped the Vichy government set up its fascist regime, including an anti-Semitic program. Darlan, in short, stood for everything the Allies were supposed to be dedicated to destroying. "What the hell are we fighting for?" liberals in Washington and London demanded. Churchill and his friends were horrified. De Gaulle was furious. He insisted that he and the Free French—not the Vichy traitors—should be at the head of the North African government. And he joined British and American critics of the Darlan Deal to raise serious questions: If the Americans were willing to deal with fascists in North Africa, did that also mean that when the Allies got into Italy they would make a deal with Mussolini? If the opportunity presented itself, would they deal with Hitler or the German generals?

Eisenhower was the subject of continuing, bitter criticism. Many commentators demanded that he be relieved of his command. Roosevelt and Churchill bombarded him with questions, demanding to know why he had dealt with Darlan in the first place and why he did not get rid of him at once. Eisenhower spent the next two weeks explaining his position. He insisted that he had had no choice, since none of the French officers had obeyed Giraud and he did not want to waste time fighting the French. He had ignored the political implications of the Darlan Deal because he wanted to concentrate on the military requirements. For the same reason, he could not dump Darlan; if he did, the French would start fighting the Allies again.

Many of Eisenhower's critics charged that he was a typical military man with a reactionary, right-wing mind. He resented such charges even more than he did the pressure from Churchill and Roosevelt. "I can't understand why these long-haired, starry-eyed guys keep gunning for me," he told a British official. "I'm no reactionary. Christ on the mountain! I'm as idealistic as Hell." To an American friend he complained, "I think sometimes that I am a cross between a one-time soldier, a pseudo-statesman, a jack-legged politician and a crooked diplomat. I walk a soapy tight-rope in a rain storm with a blazing furnace on one side and a pack of ravenous tigers on the other." If he got safely across, Ike said, his greatest possible reward would be a quiet little cottage "on the side of a slow-moving stream where I can sit and fish for catfish with a bobber."

The Darlan Deal is difficult to judge. Eisenhower had tried Giraud, but Giraud could not deliver the goods; at that point he had little choice in his search for a Frenchman who could take over the administration of Algeria and, more important, get the French colonial army to stop fighting. In the long run he would have been better off dealing with de Gaulle, but in the immediate situation that was impossible. First, Roosevelt's personal animosity toward de Gaulle was so great that the President would never have agreed to deal with him, and second, the French officers in Algeria would not have obeyed orders from de Gaulle. If Eisenhower had understood some of the political differences dividing Frenchmen he might have handled the situation more efficiently, but it is hard to see what basic changes he could have made.

After a month of tension, Roosevelt and Churchill reluctantly accepted the fact that only Darlan could make the French Army in North Africa hold its fire, and they accepted the Darlan Deal. Eisenhower stayed in command, although under orders to find some way to get rid of Darlan.

A happy solution—for the Allies—came on Christmas Eve, 1942, when a young anti-Nazi Frenchman in Algiers assassinated Darlan. The embarrassment of dealing with the Fascist was over. Eisenhower saw to it that Giraud replaced Darlan at the head of the North African government, although de Gaulle was soon able to squeeze out Giraud and assume power himself.

While Eisenhower had been dealing with the political problems, he had also handled the innumerable details involved in preparing and mounting the invasion. How well he did this nearly impossible task was summed up by Admiral Andrew Cunningham, head of the British naval forces in TORCH. Cunningham's tribute to Ike deserves to be quoted in full: "I liked him at once. He struck me as being completely sincere, straightforward and very modest. In those early days I rather had the impression that he was not very sure of himself; but who could wonder at that? He was in supreme command of one of the greatest amphibious operations of all time, and was working in a strange country with an Ally whose methods were largely unfamiliar. But as time went on Eisenhower grew quickly in stature and it was not too long before one recognized him as the really great man he is—forceful, able, direct and far-seeing, with great charm of manner, and always with a rather naive wonder at attaining the high position in which he found himself."

On the Tunisian battlefront, meanwhile, the Allies had made almost no progress. After some initial success their offensive had slowed to a complete halt, primarily be-

113

cause of unusually heavy rains, which turned the roads into deep pools of mud. The Germans took advantage of the situation to rush troops from Italy into Tunisia, so that the Allied position was growing worse instead of better. Eisenhower had spent most of his time on political problems arising from the Darlan Deal. On December 22, 1942, Marshall ordered him to "delegate your international diplomatic problems to your subordinates and give your complete attention to the battle in Tunisia." Eisenhower intended to do just that.

chapter eight

The Battle for Kasserine Pass

When the Allies invaded North Africa they caught the Germans by surprise. Eisenhower's troops moved eastward from Algeria into Tunisia; they got to within fifteen miles of the city of Tunis before the Germans, under General Jürgen von Arnim, could get a force to the front to oppose the advance. Then the rains came, more German reinforcements moved into Tunisia, and the Allies were thrown back. It would be five months before they got that close to Tunis again.

Eisenhower had two major problems. The road system in North Africa was primitive at best, the rains made it worse, and he had few trucks. Thus it was impossible for him to get supplies of food and ammunition up to the front-line troops, despite "impressing every kind of scrawny vehicle that can run." His second problem was the lack of experience—the American troops in North Africa had never been in combat. The Germans were outfighting and outthinking them. The GI's were pinned down, driven back, nearly routed. Major General Lloyd Fredendall, commanding the U.S. II Corps, had his headquarters far to the rear, seldom went to the front, had little idea of what was happening there, and in general provided poor leadership. General Kenneth Anderson, commanding the British First Army on the left (northern) flank, was not much better. Eisenhower had been so tied down by the political situation in Algiers that he had not taken a firm grip on the battle. The result was a real mess.

All through January, Eisenhower tried to straighten things out. He made frequent trips to the battlefield, encouraged Fredendall to get out of his bunker and visit the troops, urged Anderson to attack whenever possible, and begged the War Department for more trucks, tanks, airplanes, and road-building equipment. But the rains continued, turning the whole of North Africa into a deep pool of mud. Nothing could move. An aide reported that Eisenhower was "like a caged tiger, snarling and clawing to get things done."

The Germans were getting things done. Rommel had brought his Afrika Korps onto Eisenhower's front. Montgomery was on his heels, but not close enough to hamper Rommel's linkup with von Arnim. The Germans were now free to concentrate their combined force against Eisenhower's exposed troops. Rommel decided to attack the green American troops at Kasserine Pass, break through the Tunisian mountain barrier, then drive on to Algiers itself. He hoped to split the U.S. II Corps and the British First Army, then turn back on the British force and destroy it. If all went well, the Germans could drive the Allies into the sea and regain their grip on North Africa.

Eisenhower realized the dangers but, like his troops, he was new to actual combat and had much to learn. He continued to send gentle hints and suggestions to Fredendall, rather than firm orders. Although he had serious doubts about Fredendall's abilities (and those of the other senior American officers in Tunisia), he decided to give them a chance to prove themselves. Eisenhower visited Kasserine Pass, complained about the position of the troops but did nothing to change it, urged his men to be watchful, and then began a leisurely journey back to his headquarters, stopping along the way to visit the famous Roman ruins at Timgad.

While Ike was sightseeing, Rommel attacked. On February 20, 1943, his panzer tanks burst through Kasserine Pass, blowing the GI's aside and opening a wide gap in Eisenhower's line. And while American troops ran from the enemy, Fredendall remained at his headquarters, miles to the rear, issuing no orders, doing almost nothing. Anderson, meanwhile, refused to send reinforcements south because he feared a second German attack against his front.

All through February 21 and 22 Rommel raced forward. Eisenhower's subordinates wanted to pull far back and set up a new defensive line in the rear, but by the evening of the 22nd it was clear to Eisenhower that Rommel had shot his bolt. The Germans did not have enough fuel to continue the advance and in fact had placed themselves in a dangerous position, with all their supplies coming through one narrow gap in the mountains. Eisenhower wanted an immediate counterattack— his idea was that Fredendall should get behind Rommel, take Kasserine Pass, then destroy the Afrika Korps. But Fredendall insisted on a passive defense, refused to counterattack, and eventually allowed Rommel to escape. The Germans had given the GI's a good licking but had failed to win the campaign, much less drive the Allies out of North Africa.

There was a hidden blessing in the Battle for Kasserine Pass, for it was at Kasserine that Eisenhower and the American Army came of age. Rommel had wanted to scare the GI's, to convince them that they could never stand up to the mighty German Army, the Wehrmacht. But in the final phases of the battle the Americans had fought well and the GI's decided that they could, after all, take on the best the Wehrmacht had to offer. "All our people," Eisenhower reported, "from the very highest to the very lowest, have learned that this is not a child's game and are ready and eager to get down to the fundamental business of profiting by the lessons they have learned."

Eisenhower himself learned the most. From this point on he made it a fixed rule that no unit under his command would ever stop training, including units on the front line. Ike also learned to get tough with his high-ranking officers. He fired Fredendall, an intelligence officer, and a number of lesser commanders. He brought Patton from Casablanca to take command of II Corps and gave his old friend a stern lecture. "You must not retain for one instant any man in a responsible position where you have become doubtful of his ability to do the job," Eisenhower said, having in mind his own failure to relieve Fredendall earlier. "This matter frequently calls for more courage than any other thing you will have to do, but I expect you to be perfectly cold-blooded about it." Eisenhower insisted that "officers that fail must be ruthlessly weeded out. Considerations of friendship, family, kindliness and nice personality have nothing whatsoever to do with the problem." He wanted Patton to get rid of "the lazy, the slothful, the indifferent or the complacent." That was the great lesson of Kasserine Pass.

George Patton was the perfect man for the job. Hard as steel, personally ambitious, anxious to prove that the Americans could fight as well as the British, he set to work with a will. Patton shook up the whole command, put the troops through a series of tough training exercises, then launched small-scale attacks against Rommel's forces, attacks designed to build up the GIs' confidence in themselves. Patton accomplished more in two weeks than his predecessors had in four months.

By March Montgomery had brought the British Eighth Army into the battle; in combination with Patton he was driving the Germans back to their last stronghold around Tunis. (Hitler had pulled Rommel out of North Africa after Kasserine Pass; he did not want to have the popular general suffer defeat.) Satisfied with the progress, Eisenhower replaced Patton with his old friend and West Point classmate, Omar Bradley. Ike told Patton to prepare for the invasion of Sicily, scheduled to begin when North Africa was cleared of the enemy.

By mid-April, 1943, the German fate in North Africa was sealed. Anderson on the left, or northern flank, Bradley in the center, and Montgomery on the right, or southern flank, were pressing the Germans hard. With his back to the sea, von Arnim had no place to go. Since the linkup between the American forces and the British Eighth Army, Eisenhower had been the overall commander for the Allied armed forces in North Africa; General Harold Alexander, a British officer, was his

119

*George Patton—
the toughest fighting
man on Ike's team.*

ground forces commander. As the Allies prepared for the final assault, Alexander told Eisenhower that he wanted to take the American troops out of the line, leaving the last battle to the British troops under Generals Anderson and Montgomery. Alexander feared that the GI's were not good enough to assault German troops in prepared defensive positions and he wanted the experienced British soldiers to deliver the final blow.

Eisenhower absolutely refused. He told Alexander that North Africa was only a beginning, and not much of a beginning at that, considering the relatively small number of German troops engaged in the battle. When the Allies invaded the continent of Europe they would be taking on far greater numbers of German troops and they would need every man they could put on the firing line. Those additional men could only come from America—Britain was already fully engaged. Eisenhower admitted that for the short run it might be better to leave the last phase of the African campaign to the British, but in the long run it would be disastrous. If the GI's were not confident of their ability to defeat the Germans, they would not be up to the job to come. Far from pulling the GI's out of the line, Eisenhower told Alexander to give them the toughest objective in Tunisia.

Alexander did. He told Bradley to take Hill 609, the best-defended position in Tunisia and the key to the German line. If Bradley could break through at Hill 609 he would rout the Wehrmacht. Eisenhower ordered Bradley to do whatever he had to in order to take the hill. "We have reached the point where troops *must* secure objectives assigned," Eisenhower said.

The GI's did the job. On April 30 they attacked Hill 609; after a fierce and bloody battle they drove the Germans from their positions and opened a great gap in von Arnim's line. Montgomery attacked from the south, Anderson from the northwest, and by early May the Germans were in full retreat. On May 7 Bradley sent Eisenhower a two-word message—"Mission accomplished." A week later the last German stragglers surrendered. Eisenhower's forces had captured 275,000 enemy troops, a bag of prisoners even larger than the Russians had taken at Stalingrad earlier in the year.

Eisenhower had spent the last week of the campaign at the front, and it made a deep impression on him. He spoke of it in a letter to his brother Arthur. Ike had just learned that a reporter had done a story on their mother; the story stressed her pacifism and the irony of Mrs. Eisenhower's son being a general. After telling Arthur that their mother's "happiness in her religion means more to me than any damn wisecrack that a newspaperman can get publicized," Ike said of pacifists generally, "I doubt whether any of these people, with their academic or dogmatic hatred of war, detest it as much as I do." Pacifists, he said, "probably have not seen bodies rotting on the ground and smelled the stench of decaying human flesh. They have not visited a field hospital crowded with the desperately wounded." Ike said that what separated him from the pacifists was that he hated the Nazis more than he did war.

The forces under Eisenhower's command had cleared North Africa of the enemy. The Allies now controlled the sea lanes in the Mediterranean. Germany had not been struck a mortal blow, but it had been hurt. More important, Ike had put together a team of proven commanders, led by Bradley, Patton, and Montgomery. The GI's had learned to take on and overcome the best the Wehrmacht had to offer, while Ike himself discovered how tough the business of command in war really was. At the beginning of the campaign he had been far too soft on his subordinates; now he was prepared to fire any general, immediately, if he did not produce results. The Allies were now ready to carry the war more directly to the enemy.

Ike and Patton map reference points during the Tunisian cam-paign. Patton has just taken over the U.S. II Corps.

After the German surrender in Tunisia, congratulations poured in on Ike from all sides—from the President, the Prime Minister, British and American generals and admirals, and from soldiers, sailors, and private citizens throughout the world. Ike claimed not to be impressed. He said he could not relax and enjoy a feeling of self-satisfaction, for "I always anticipate and discount, in my own mind, accomplishment, and am, therefore, mentally racing ahead into the next campaign. The consequence is that all the shouting about the Tunisian campaign leaves me utterly cold." He had already started to think about the invasion of Sicily.

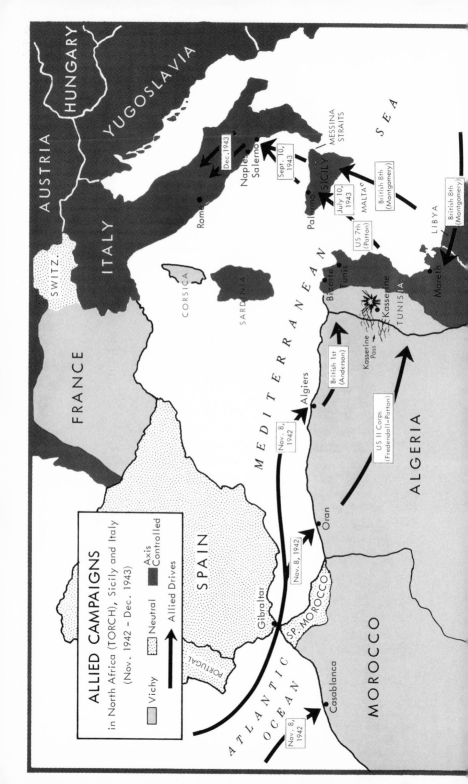

ALLIED CAMPAIGNS
in North Africa (TORCH), Sicily and Italy
(Nov. 1942 – Dec. 1943)

Allied Drives

Neutral

Vichy

Axis Controlled

AUSTRIA

HUNGARY

YUGOSLAVIA

SWITZ.

FRANCE

ITALY

Dec.1943

Rome

Naples
Salerno

Sept. 10, 1943

CORSICA

SARDINIA

M E D I T E R R A N E A N

MESSINA STRAITS

SICILY

Palermo

July 10, 1943

MALTA

S E A

British 8th (Montgomery)

US 7th (Patton)

Bizerte
Tunis

Kasserine

TUNISIA

Kasserine Pass

Mareth

LIBYA

British 8th (Montgomery)

Algiers

British 1st (Anderson)

Nov. 8, 1942

Oran

Nov. 8, 1942

US II Corps
(Fredendall–Patton)

ALGERIA

SPAIN

PORTUGAL

Gibraltar

SP. MOROCCO

MOROCCO

Casablanca

Nov. 8, 1942

A T L A N T I C

O C E A N

chapter nine
Sicily and Italy

Following his success in North Africa in 1943, Ike went
into a period of intensive work, preparing for the invasion of Sicily. Although he was now an experienced commander of amphibious forces and could handle most of
the difficulties easily, there were added problems, since
this was to be a much larger operation—the invasion of
Sicily would become the biggest amphibious attack in
the history of man, even larger in its initial stages than
the invasion of France in 1944 would be. Eisenhower
also spent a great deal of time on French political affairs; after a long and complex series of arguments, he
finally persuaded Roosevelt to allow de Gaulle to take
command of the French government in North Africa. Ike
was the best friend de Gaulle had in the Allied camp;
had it not been for Ike, the sensitive and proud leader of
Free France might have refused to cooperate with the
Allies throughout the remainder of the war.

But although politics took much of his time, Eisenhower's major concern was military. The attack on Sicily was scheduled to begin on July 10, 1943, with Montgomery landing on the right flank, Patton on the left. Preparations went smoothly until D-Day minus one—July 9—when the weather turned bad. The wind roared in from the west, piling up whitecaps in the Mediterranean, tossing about the fragile landing craft in which Patton's men were crossing, and throwing a heavy surf on the Sicilian beaches. Staff officers suggested that Eisenhower postpone the invasion before it was too late. Because of the size and complexity of the forces involved, such a postponement would have meant a two- or three-week delay before the invasion could be mounted again.

Ike was the one man who could decide. At his headquarters on the island of Malta in the Mediterranean he consulted with weather experts, who predicted that the wind would diminish around sundown. Marshall sent a wire asking if the invasion was on or off. Eisenhower exclaimed, "I wish I knew!" He went outside to check weather conditions, listened to the weather experts repeat their favorable prediction, rubbed his ever-present seven lucky coins, and silently prayed for the safety and success of all the men under his command.

Then he went inside and announced that the operation would go as scheduled. Now the brass hats could only wait and hope the weathermen were right. They played cards and chatted to kill time. Hours later someone turned on a little table radio and picked up a program of the British Broadcasting Corporation. Eisenhower and his aides gathered around it to wait for the latest news—

it seemed the best way of finding out when and if the troops got ashore, since the ships were maintaining radio silence. The BBC was playing popular music. Eisenhower began pacing the floor. Suddenly the announcer said, "We interrupt this programme to give you a flash message from General Eisenhower—he reports that the first waves of his landing craft have just landed successfully in Sicily."

Ike looked at the others, grinned, and said, "Thank God—*he* ought to know."

The invasion worked, partly because the wind eased off, partly because the Italian troops defending the island had no real interest in Mussolini's war, nor could they see any point in laying down their lives for the sake of Nazi Germany. They surrendered in droves. There were two German divisions of between 10,000 and 15,000 men each in Sicily; their aim was to slow the Allied advance as much as possible and to make certain that they held the Messina Straits, which gave them an escape route to the Italian mainland. Montgomery pushed forward on the right, attempting to get to Messina before the Germans established a defensive position there, but he had to go around Mount Etna on the eastern end of Sicily and his progress was slow. Patton, meanwhile, dashed off to capture Sicily's largest city, Palermo. Patton pushed his tanks hard and earned the headlines; the trouble was that the Germans were still holding up Montgomery and keeping their escape route open. Eisenhower told Patton to drive on to Messina, but Patton's progress was slow in the mountain area, which was defended by crack German troops.

As Patton's tanks roll through Sicily in July, 1943, townspeople shout, "Long live America." Italy's government was allied with Germany, but most Italians just wanted out of the war.

On August 10 Patton visited a forward hospital. He was almost beside himself because of the slowness of the advance. After talking with some of the wounded men, he saw a soldier who apparently had nothing wrong with him. Patton asked what the trouble was. The soldier replied, "It's my nerves," and began to sob. Patton lost his self-control and screamed, "What did you say?"

"It's my nerves. I can't stand the shelling anymore." He continued to sob. "Your nerves, hell," Patton yelled. "You are just a goddamn coward, you yellow son of a bitch." He slapped the man's face, hard. "Shut up that goddamn crying. I won't have these brave men here, who have been shot, seeing a yellow bastard sitting here crying." He slapped the man again and ordered the doctors to put him back on the front line.

In the United States Army it is a highly serious offense for an officer to hit an enlisted man. Word of the slapping incident spread quickly, even though Patton's superiors tried to hush it up. A week later Eisenhower learned of the incident. "If this thing ever gets out," Ike said, "they'll be howling for Patton's scalp, and that will be the end of Georgie's service in this war. I simply cannot let that happen. Patton is *indispensable* to the war effort—one of the guarantors of our victory."

Eisenhower wanted to keep the incident quiet, but he also needed to make sure that nothing like it happened again. He wrote a stern letter to Patton, saying he could understand why his friend had lost his temper but pointing out that "this does not excuse brutality, abuse of the sick, nor exhibition of uncontrollable temper in front of subordinates." He told Patton that next time he would send him back to the States in disgrace, and he ordered Patton to apologize to the soldier he had struck and to the nurses and doctors in the forward hospital. It came hard to the proud Patton, but he made the apology. That seemed to be the end of it, but the story later leaked to the press. Again Eisenhower protected Patton. He knew Patton's shortcomings better than anyone else, and handling the wild, unpredictable, coarse Patton was no easy job. But Patton could keep troops moving forward and the enemy off balance when no one else could do the job. When the decisive test came, Eisenhower wanted Patton at his side.

By mid-August, Sicily had been cleared of the enemy, but Eisenhower had no opportunity to relax. He was already preparing for the invasion of the Italian mainland while simultaneously dealing with complex political problems brought about by the recent fall of Mussolini.

In late July, at Eisenhower's insistence, the Allies had bombed Rome. The shock to the Italians was so great that the Italian legislature held a special meeting, overthrew and arrested Mussolini (who was also blamed for the loss of Sicily), and set up a new government under Pietro Badoglio. Badoglio, in turn, approached the Allies through secret missions, hoping to double-cross the Germans. Badoglio wanted to surrender to the Allies, then join them in the war against Germany. Italy, in other words, wanted to be on the winning side in the war, and now assumed that was the Allied side.

Eisenhower was anxious to make a deal. If the Allies cooperated with Badoglio they could get control of Italy without having to lose men in a bitter military campaign.

His political superiors, however, felt differently. Roosevelt and Churchill were terrified at the prospect of another Darlan Deal—Badoglio was as much a Fascist as Mussolini—and the effect it would have on public opinion on the home fronts. In North Africa, Eisenhower had been able to act, then inform his bosses; in Italy they made sure he did nothing about politics without their approval. Consequently, great opportunities were lost.

The chief difficulty was the Allied demand for unconditional surrender. After the Darlan Deal, Roosevelt had announced that there would be no more compromises with the Fascists—instead the Allies would insist on the unconditional surrender of their enemies. For Badoglio and the Italians, however, unconditional surrender was much too bitter a pill. They wanted to hurry through a simple surrender ceremony, then immediately announce that they had joined the Allied team. Badoglio would remain in power. Eisenhower was on Badoglio's side, for the sole reason that he did not want to waste men fighting for control of Italy. But he could not convince Churchill and Roosevelt, who continued to insist on unconditional surrender and to keep a close watch on Ike's every move. He told an aide he wished they were back in the days of sailing ships, when generals in the field operated under broad directives and took care of all the details themselves.

There were two other complicating factors. First, the Italians had no freedom of movement, since the Germans had a few divisions stationed in and around Rome. If the Germans found out that the Italians were planning to double-cross them, they could take control of the city, for the Italian Army was in sad shape and incapable of defending itself, much less the capital. Second, Eisenhower himself had relatively few troops available. He was planning the invasion of Italy on a shoestring, for by mid-1943, the Allies were concentrating on building up their forces in England for the 1944 invasion of Europe. There were no spare troops available for Italy.

Under the circumstances, Badoglio wanted Eisenhower to drive the Germans out of Italy for him, while Eisenhower wanted the Italian Army to do the job. Neither man knew how militarily weak the other really was; each tried to hide his weakness. Badoglio thought Eisenhower was going to land near Rome with twenty divisions, while in fact Ike was preparing to land far south of Rome, at Salerno, with only three divisions. Eisenhower thought the Italian Army could still fight, which Badoglio knew was impossible, so low was his army's morale. In the meantime the two men were trying to work out a surrender formula that would not be too embarrassing to the Italians, but stern enough to satisfy Roosevelt and Churchill. It was a maddening process and they made little progress.

The invasion of mainland Italy was scheduled for September 9, 1943. Two days earlier, Eisenhower sent General Maxwell Taylor on a secret mission to Rome. Taylor traveled by PT boat to the Italian coast, then drove to the city in an Italian Army vehicle under pretext of being a prisoner of war. His purpose was to arrange for a landing by American paratroopers at the Rome airfield. Eisenhower did not want to risk an entire airborne division unless he was certain the Italians could keep the Germans away from the airfield; Badoglio did not want to announce publicly that he had switched sides in the war unless the Allies could protect him from the Germans. Taylor discovered that Badoglio had no forces available to hold the airfield; Badoglio discovered that the Allies were not coming in anything like the force he expected, nor were they landing close enough to Rome to satisfy him.

Badoglio demanded postponement of the invasion. Taylor argued with him all night long, and finally gave up. He flashed a radio message to Eisenhower, telling him to call off the airborne operation. The message got through just in time—the planes had already left Sicily and were on their way when they received word to return to base. Badoglio then said that he would not make the announcement his representatives and Eisenhower had agreed upon—an announcement that would take Italy out of the war without settling any of the vexing questions about the nature of her surrender.

When he heard that Badoglio was backing down, Ike went livid. The Allied Commander immediately threatened to tell the Germans everything if Badoglio did not go through with his part of the deal. The Germans would learn that the Italians had been meeting secretly with the Allies and had decided to declare war on Germany. The Nazis would then place Badoglio under arrest, take control of Rome, and treat Italy as just another occupied country. Eisenhower's threat was sufficient—on the morning of the invasion Badoglio made the promised announcement. Ike grunted with satisfaction; he said he had "played a little poker" and won.

It turned out that all the fuss was over nothing. It hardly mattered which side Italy was on, the Italian Army was so weak and depressed. It made no attempt to resist the Germans who rushed into Italy to take control; it did not even put up a fight for Rome. Within a matter of days Hitler had twenty divisions stationed south of Rome, so though the Allied invasion at Salerno was a success, the troops were unable to break out of their beachhead.

It took the Allies nearly a year to get to Rome; Eisenhower had hoped to take it during the first days of the campaign. The Germans fought ferociously and took intelligent advantage of the natural mountain defenses, while the Allies never had enough men or planes to force a breakthrough. Eisenhower always felt that the campaign could have been avoided if his political masters had allowed him to deal with Badoglio as he wished, in which case his troops probably could have occupied Rome before the Germans got there. It is, of course, impossible to judge whether he was right or wrong; what is certain is that American and British soldiers paid a bloody price to take Italy.

In November the troops did move forward far enough to allow Eisenhower to establish an advanced command post on the Continent, in the Caserta Palace north of Naples. This was a fancy hunting lodge, and Ike's aides were proud of their discovery. When Ike arrived, an aide filled him with stories about the attractive features of the palace. But the General had hardly entered when someone came running downstairs with the news that there was a rat in Ike's bathroom. Ike took personal command. Pulling a revolver, he marched into the bathroom and fired four shots. All missed. A staff officer finally killed the rat with a stick. They then got into the elevator, where they got stuck and stood around for half an hour waiting to be freed. The fireplace in Ike's bedroom did not work and there were lice in the beds. An aide commented, "It's a tough war."

The Americans in Italy showed a conqueror's mentality, moving the Italians out of their homes and taking possession for themselves. On a cruise around the Isle of Capri on Christmas Eve, 1943, Eisenhower spotted a large villa. "Whose is that?" he asked. "Yours, sir," someone replied—an aide had arranged it. Nodding at another, even larger, villa, Ike asked, "And that?" "That one belongs to General Spaatz," was the answer. (General Carl Spaatz was the head of the American Air Forces in Italy.)

"Damn it," Ike exploded, "that's *not* my villa! And that's not General Spaatz's villa! None of those will belong to any general as long as I'm boss around here. This is supposed to be a rest center—for combat men—not a playground for the brass!"

He was not just putting on an act. When he got back to shore he investigated, found that Spaatz had reserved Capri as a recreation facility for Air Force officers; he exploded again. "This is directly contrary to my policies and must cease at once," he told Spaatz, and ordered him to see to it immediately that "all British and American personnel in this area, particularly from combat units, may be assured of proportionate opportunity in taking advantage of these facilities."

The Capri story and other similar stories quickly got out to the troops and delighted them. Nothing pleased the footslogger struggling in the mud of Italy more than hearing that Ike had put Spaatz or some other general in his place. The fact that Ike often referred to Churchill, Roosevelt, and the Combined Chiefs as the "big shots," or that he swore like a sergeant, was much appreciated by the men. So were his frequent visits to the front lines, especially because he listened to the troops' complaints and, when he could, did something about them. His popularity with the men rested on his genuine concern for their welfare and on his common touch—they regarded him as one of them.

But although morale was high, progress was slow.

At the front a combination of rain, poor mountain roads, and extremely effective German defenses held up the advance, which in truth was little more than a crawl. Eisenhower fretted and fumed, but nothing he could do could get the offensive rolling. Meanwhile he had to carry on a long strategic debate with Churchill. The Prime Minister now wanted Eisenhower to send men, ships, and planes to drive the Germans out of Greece and, possibly, to open another front in the Balkans. Eisenhower, Marshall, and the Americans generally regarded this proposition as simply another attempt on Churchill's part to postpone or even eliminate the scheduled 1944 invasion of France. Eisenhower resisted all of Churchill's impassioned pleas, but it wore him out. The result was that no new front was opened; the Allies remained committed to the invasion of France.

They were, unfortunately, unable to make any progress in Italy. Montgomery hoped to start a big offensive thrust in early December, but torrential rains made movement impossible. The American troops in Italy were also stalled. Eisenhower made a series of trips to the front, inspected the positions, talked to officers and men, and brought in what supplies he could, but could not get the offensive rolling. The Germans—and the weather—had imposed a stalemate in Italy.

chapter ten

Preparing OVERLORD

By the fall of 1943 the Allies were centering their efforts on Operation OVERLORD, the invasion of France from England across the Channel. Even in Italy, Eisenhower had to conduct his offensive in such a fashion as to help OVERLORD; one major objective had been to capture airfields from which Allied bombers could reach targets in Germany and France. For the next eight months the human and material resources of two great nations would be directed toward the single objective of mounting an amphibious assault on a small bit of the coast of western France.

Command of OVERLORD was the most coveted in the war, perhaps in all history. The commander would have tremendous forces at his disposal. If the operation worked he could probably take much of the credit for defeating Nazi Germany. No reward, not even the Presidency itself, would be too great for the successful commander of OVERLORD.

President Roosevelt, as head of the nation making the largest contribution of men and supplies to OVERLORD, would choose the commander. Most observers assumed it would be George Marshall, for OVERLORD was Marshall's brainchild. He had been the first to suggest it and had fought for it since the war began. If Roosevelt picked Marshall, then Eisenhower would have to go somewhere else; having an American in command of the Northwestern European theater meant that, to keep the Allies in balance, a British officer would have to take charge of the Mediterranean theater. Ike expected to go back to Washington to become Marshall's replacement as Chief of Staff. The prospect hardly appealed to him. Ike wanted command of one of the American armies operating under Marshall in OVERLORD.

Rumors about who was going where filled Army offices from Washington to Algiers. In October, Eisenhower sent his right-hand man and Chief of Staff, Walter B. Smith, to Washington to talk with Marshall. Ike wanted Smith to discuss problems in the Italian offensive, but he also asked Smith to find out about the OVERLORD command. He told Smith not to raise the subject, but if Marshall brought it up, Ike wanted Smith to make it clear that his personal desire was to command in the field, under Marshall. Even if Marshall did not bring up his future, Ike "naturally hoped that Smith would find the lay of the land." While Smith was gone an aide reported that Eisenhower was "sweating it out in big drops. This uncertainty takes the pep out of everyone."

Smith returned in early November. He reported that Marshall was to go to OVERLORD on January 1, 1944, with Eisenhower taking his place as Chief of Staff in Washington. Ike was disappointed. He wanted to tell President Roosevelt that it was a "tremendous mistake," for he was "not temperamentally fitted for the job." He feared it would destroy him. Eisenhower knew that he had no patience with politicians because he could not bear to continue an argument "after logic had made the opposition's position untenable, yet politicians persist against all logic," and the U.S. Chief of Staff spends much of his time with politicians. All this was just letting steam off with his aides, however; when the time came, Eisenhower would obey orders without complaint or question.

On November 20 Roosevelt stopped off in North Africa on his way to Cairo, Egypt, where he was soon to meet with Churchill and the CCS. Eisenhower joined him in Tunis and took the President on a tour of the battlefield sites, both recent and ancient. While they were riding in a jeep, Roosevelt told Eisenhower that he dreaded the thought of losing Marshall in Washington, but added, "You and I know the name of the Chief of Staff in the Civil War, but few Americans outside the professional services do." The President was afraid that if Marshall did not command OVERLORD his name would be lost to history. Eisenhower assured Roosevelt that he would do the best he could at whatever job he was given.

After the Cairo meeting, Roosevelt and Churchill went on to Teheran, Iran, for their first wartime meeting with Premier Joseph Stalin. The Russian leader was deeply suspicious of the Allies; he feared they were not serious about opening a second front in France and indeed were willing to watch Russia and Germany destroy each other.

Since Eisenhower's forces in Italy were fighting about twenty German divisions, while the Red Army had nearly three hundred divisions to contend with, Stalin's view, naturally, was that the Allies were not doing their share in the common war against the Nazis. Roosevelt and Churchill talked grandly about OVERLORD in an attempt to ease Stalin's suspicions, but the Russian went right to the heart of the matter when he said he would never believe the Allies were serious about OVERLORD until they appointed a commander for the operation. "Who will it be?" Stalin demanded, looking directly at Roosevelt. The President squirmed, muttered that he could not make up his mind, and brought the meeting to an end.

Roosevelt's hesitancy came from his unwillingness to lose Marshall's services as Chief of Staff. He remarked that he could not sleep at night with Marshall out of Washington. Marshall's job was too big and too important to sacrifice him for anything, even OVERLORD. When it came to the crunch, Roosevelt had to have Marshall at his side.

In early December, 1943, Roosevelt and Churchill met in Cairo; Marshall was there too. The President made his decision. He asked Marshall to write a message to Stalin. As Roosevelt dictated, Marshall wrote. "From the President to Marshal Stalin," it began. "The immediate appointment of General Eisenhower to command of OVERLORD operation has been decided upon." Roosevelt then signed it.

It was, perhaps, a thoughtless and cruel way to inform Marshall that he had lost his historic opportunity, but there was no way the President could have done it easily.

142

Marshall never expressed the slightest disappointment and he never complained. The next morning, in fact, he retrieved his original handwritten draft from the radio room. At the bottom, Marshall scribbled, "Dear Eisenhower. I thought you might like to have this as a memento," and sent it to Ike. Eisenhower framed it and for the rest of his life kept it in a prominent position on his office wall.

An intimate associate of the President's felt it was "one of the most difficult and one of the loneliest decisions he [Roosevelt] ever had to make." In the field of appointments, it was also one of his best.

Eisenhower spent early January, 1944, in the States with Mamie—his only vacation during the entire war—then flew to London on January 14 to take command of OVERLORD. Somewhat to his surprise, he found that he was now a world figure, known to everyone on the streets and constantly pestered by newspaper reporters. Having never been famous before, he hardly knew how to respond to all the attention, so he just did what came most naturally—he was himself. He talked straight to the reporters, told them what his problems were, what he hoped might happen, outlined his general ideas, and most of all remained warm, friendly, and truthful. The reporters, accustomed to dealing with big-shot VIP's, loved it. They gave him marvelous write-ups and helped make him the most popular general in the Allied world.

Eisenhower acted the same way with the troops. He realized that no matter how well the high command did its job, in the end everything depended on the GI's and British Tommies on the firing line. If they did well, the

Allies would win; if not, defeat was entirely possible. So Ike spent much of his time visiting the various Allied divisions training all across Britain. He would have the men gather around him, tell them to sit down and relax, then encourage them to keep training. He let them know what he expected of them, and pointed out that the sooner they licked the Wehrmacht, the sooner they could go home. When he finished he would walk out into the crowd and exchange a few words with individuals, listening to their complaints, telling jokes, letting the men get to know their commander. He tried to meet and talk with each of the men who would be going ashore in the first wave of OVERLORD. It meant a lot to the troops.

Eisenhower also tried to get the troops to recognize the meaning of the war. He felt strongly that the Allied cause was an inspiring one, and he thought that every commander had a responsibility to make the issues clear to the men. The GI and the Tommy had to be made to realize that "the privileged life he has led . . . is under direct threat. His right to speak his own mind, to belong to any religious denomination, to live in any locality where he can support himself and his family, and to be sure of fair treatment when he might be accused of any crime—all these would disappear if the forces opposed to us should, through carelessness or overconfidence on our part, succeed in winning this war." To Eisenhower, the Allied cause was "completely bound up with the rights and welfare of the common man."

Eisenhower handpicked his subordinates for OVER-LORD, taking most of them from the Mediterranean theater.

144

At SHAEF headquarters, Ike is flanked by his British Deputy Supreme Commander, Arthur Tedder, and General Bernard Montgomery. Standing (left to right): *Bradley; naval commander Bertram Ramsay; chief of the fighter air forces Trafford Leigh-Mallory; and Walter B. Smith.*

Churchill had wanted him to leave Smith in Italy to help the new commander there, but Eisenhower insisted on having Smith for his Chief of Staff at Supreme Headquarters, Allied Expeditionary Force (SHAEF). Air Marshal Arthur Tedder, the British officer who had been head of the air forces in North Africa, became Deputy Supreme Commander. Montgomery would command the ground forces; Bradley would command the American

Army in the first assault, then become an Army Group commander when the second American army crossed the English Channel and joined the battle. Eisenhower's own title was lofty—Supreme Commander, Allied Expeditionary Force. All the men at SHAEF pitched in with a will; as Eisenhower put it, at SHAEF there was "a very deep conviction, in all circles, that we are approaching a tremendous crisis with stakes incalculable." In his first report on OVERLORD to the CCS, Eisenhower declared that "every obstacle must be overcome, every inconvenience suffered and every risk run to ensure that our blow is decisive. We cannot afford to fail."

The first problem was to select an invasion site in France. The requirements were complex. The landings had to come at a spot within range of fighter planes based in Britain and within an overnight sailing distance for ships from the southern ports of England. There had to be a nearby port for unloading equipment. The beach had to be firm enough to hold tanks rumbling inland with the invading troops. Calais was the obvious target area, since it was the closest French port to England, but this was as clear to the Germans as it was to the Allies, so German defenses at Calais were strong. That left the Normandy area. It had a good port at Cherbourg, it was close enough to Britain, and it was protected from the most extreme Atlantic storms by the Cotentin Peninsula.

With Normandy selected, Eisenhower's next problem was the time of the attack. It had to come at low tide, because the Germans had covered the area between the high and low water marks with steel obstacles topped with mines. Any landing craft trying to cross the area

146

would be blown up; only by attacking at low tide could Allied engineers clear the mines before the water covered them. The attack had to come at dawn so that the invasion fleet could cross the Channel under cover of darkness and the troops would have a full day to get established on the beachhead. There had to be a moon so that the pilots carrying the paratroopers—who would land behind the beaches to attack the Germans from the rear—could see where to drop them.

These conditions of low tide at first light following a moonlit night would be met only three times in the spring of 1944—during the first few days of May and the first and third weeks of June. The CCS had set May 1 as the target date, but Eisenhower selected June 4 for D-Day because he wanted his troops to have plenty of time for training.

Another vexing question for Ike was the proper use of air power. The Allies had already taken command of the air over Europe by defeating the German Luftwaffe in innumerable battles, but there was disagreement over how best to use that superiority. In general, the British and American airmen wanted to concentrate on bombing targets deep inside Germany. This was called strategic bombing, and the more aggressive airmen even claimed that if they could go all out against Germany's oil refineries and other industrial targets, they could force Germany to surrender without having to invade Europe. Air Marshal Tedder, however, convinced Eisenhower that the bombers would only be helpful to OVERLORD if they hit transportation targets in France—that is, by destroying railroads, bridges, and highways, the Allies would make it impossible for the Wehrmacht to move reserves to Normandy. Otherwise, once the Germans knew where the invasion was coming they could bring panzer and infantry divisions to Normandy and throw Eisenhower's comparatively small invasion force back into the sea.

Eisenhower agreed with Tedder. As Supreme Commander he had under him all the troops and ships involved in the OVERLORD invasion, plus the fighter airplanes necessary to give air cover over the beach—but *not* the big bombers. The big-bomber pilots, the strategic airmen, wanted to fight their own war and had told the CCS that they did not want to serve under Ike's command; they wished to remain independent. A group of big-bomber generals told Eisenhower that they "hoped OVERLORD would meet with every success, but were sorry that they could not give direct assistance because, of course, they were more than fully occupied on the really important war against Germany."

Eisenhower believed that without help from the bombers he might as well call off OVERLORD. After all, he was preparing to invade a well-defended coastline— Hitler called it his Atlantic Fortress—with fewer troops than the Germans had in Normandy already. The Wehrmacht had fifty-eight divisions in France; Ike would be invading with only five. If the Germans could bring reinforcements into Normandy, OVERLORD was doomed. So strongly did Eisenhower feel about the issue that for the first time in the war he threatened to resign if he did not get his way—specifically, if he did not get command of the big bombers. His threat did the trick—the CCS gave him command of the strategic air force.

Eisenhower sent the bombers to work at once, picking railroad targets for them throughout France. The results were spectacular. By D-Day the bombers had destroyed the great bulk of the French railroad system and much of the highway network. The Army's official historian later concluded that by D-Day the French transportation system was "on the point of total collapse" and this was "to prove critical in the battle for Normandy." Later Eisenhower said that the Transportation Plan, as the bombing program was called, had been the decisive factor in his victory at Normandy.

Eisenhower had other difficulties. For example, Churchill wanted to go along on the first wave of the invasion, and ultimately Ike had to get the King of England to stop him. Also, SHAEF did not have enough landing craft. De Gaulle and the Free French created countless problems (but contributed great benefits too, for Eisenhower counted on the French Resistance fighters behind German lines to blow bridges and tunnels when D-Day came). Then, there was not enough food in Britain, and SHAEF had to arrange to get more brought in. Secrecy was nearly impossible to maintain, but essential to success—Ike fired two senior commanders for talking about OVERLORD to unauthorized personnel. One way or another, each of these problems came to the Supreme Commander for a final decision. It put an enormous strain on him, but he held up well.

As D-Day approached Eisenhower moved his headquarters to the south of England; from here the mighty host would set sail for the great invasion. He thought he had everything well in hand, but then bad weather set in, forcing him to postpone the operation from June 4 to

Omar Bradley (center), *a quiet, modest man, always did every-thing Ike expected—and more. Because of his concern for his troops, he was often called the "GI's General." Ike considered him America's best field soldier; the two men were together in Tunisia, Sicily, Normandy, at the Battle of the Bulge and on through the victories in Germany.*

June 6. It was nerve-racking, and it did not help when the tactical air commander, British officer Trafford Leigh-Mallory, told Ike at the last minute that he wanted the paratrooper operation called off. Leigh-Mallory said that intelligence information indicated that the Germans were reinforcing the area where the U.S. 82nd Airborne Division was going to drop. He feared a "futile slaughter" of thousands of fine American boys—as many as eighty percent would become casualties, he said, and as the units would not be able to do their jobs, the men would die in vain. Eisenhower checked with Bradley, who insisted that OVERLORD would never work without the paratroopers.

As Eisenhower later put it, "It would be difficult to conceive of a more soul-racking problem." Ike went to his tent, alone, and thought about the alternatives. If he called off the airdrop, he would have to call off Bradley's landing. But then he might as well call off OVERLORD, for Montgomery's land forces could never do the job alone. If he went ahead with the airdrop and Leigh-Mallory's prediction of losses proved correct, OVERLORD would end in bloody failure. He decided the greater risk lay in cancellation, went to the telephone, and told Leigh-Mallory to go ahead with the airborne operation as scheduled. Ike would take personal responsibility. Just before the paratroopers took off for France, Eisenhower visited them, doing his best to calm the men down.

One of Eisenhower's great assets was his willingness to make the tough decisions and then accept the responsibility. After the planes carrying the paratroopers roared off for France, he sat at a portable table and scrawled a press release on a pad of paper, to be used if necessary:

"Our landings in the Cherbourg-Havre area have failed to gain a satisfactory foothold and I have withdrawn the troops," he began, hoping it would never happen that way but prepared to take the blame if it did. ". . . My decision to attack at this time and place was based upon the best information available. The troops, the air and the Navy did all that bravery and devotion to duty could do. If any blame or fault attaches to the attempt it is mine alone." He then stuffed the note in his wallet and forgot about it. Nearly a month later he happened to pull it out, chuckled over it, and started to throw it away. An aide saved it for history.

chapter eleven

The Trouble with Monty

June 6, 1944—D-Day. The Allies were ashore in France.
Bradley's and Montgomery's men had done their job, and
fortunately Leigh-Mallory's prediction had been wrong:
the paratroopers had not suffered excessive casualties.
OVERLORD had begun successfully. If Eisenhower's men
could secure the beachhead, then drive inland for the
liberation of France, Hitler's fate would be sealed. With
OVERLORD, the Germans were now forced to fight a two-
front war; they did not have sufficient manpower to do
it for long. The Wehrmacht had to pinch off the OVER-
LORD beachhead, or at least prevent any expansion of it;
Eisenhower's task was to widen the beachhead, then break
through the German lines and drive for the Rhine River.

During the first week after D-Day, the Allies poured
additional men and equipment into Normandy, gradually
increased the size of the beachhead, and fought off scattered German counterattacks. On June 12 the Allied

Chiefs of Staff, led by Marshall, came to Normandy to see things themselves. If that much brass could safely go ashore in France, the beachhead was clearly secure. Eisenhower now had ten divisions in Normandy, with more coming in each day. What Churchill rightly called "the most difficult and complicated operation that has ever taken place" had put the Allies on the continent of Europe.

They had not, however, gotten very far inland. Montgomery had promised to take Caen, the major city in the area and the gateway to Paris, on the first day of OVER-LORD, but as June gave way to July his British and Canadian troops were still outside Caen. The mood at SHAEF changed from one of exultation over the success of D-Day to one of deep concern over the lack of progress. At the heart of the difficulty was the Eisenhower-Montgomery relationship.

The two men could not have been more different. Eisenhower liked company, enjoyed being with people, worked best when he was surrounded by chattering aides, and did all that he could to make those around him happy. Montgomery lived in isolation in a lonely camp, where he slept and ate alone in a wood-paneled trailer he had captured from Rommel. Monty had shunned the company of women after his wife's death, did not smoke or drink, and never mixed easily with "the boys." Ike was

D-Day, June 6, 1944. In gray dawn and icy water (above), *infantrymen struggle down the ramp toward a Normandy beach. Up ahead, buddies duck fire from German coastal batteries.* (Below) : *GI's push ashore in a rubber lifeboat.*

an athlete with powerful muscles and a strong constitution; Monty was physically small and appeared weak. Where Ike was modest, Monty was conceited. Ike never pulled rank or put on airs, while Monty always seemed to be talking down to people. While Ike was open-minded, eager to seek out compromise, and an expert at convincing others of the correctness of his judgments, Monty had no idea in the world of how to bring others around to his point of view.

Adding to the troubles caused by their sharply different personalities, Eisenhower and Montgomery were poles apart in their strategic and tactical views. Ike believed in attacking all along his front with every available man, keeping the pressure on the Germans until they cracked somewhere. Monty wanted to hold with one part of his line, attack with a concentrated force at another point to cut through the German defenses, and dash on to his objective.

These differences came into the open during the time of the Normandy campaign. Eisenhower wanted Montgomery to attack every day, while Monty instead went on the defensive around Caen, hoping to draw the bulk of the enemy force onto that front. Montgomery's plan was to use up German reserves outside Caen by meeting and stopping their counterattacks; meanwhile the American troops under Bradley (at this time under Montgomery's overall command) would break out of Normandy and march on Paris. It was a good plan, even brilliant, and in the end it brought about one of the great victories of military history—but unfortunately Monty never explained it clearly to Ike. Indeed, Monty made things worse by pretending to follow Ike's orders when, in fact, he was doing something quite different.

A question immediately arises: Why didn't Eisenhower fire Montgomery? A number of high-ranking officers at SHAEF, including Tedder, Ike's Deputy Supreme Commander, wanted him to do just that. But things were not that simple. First, Ike did not have the authority—he had operational but not administrative command of the British forces, which meant he could tell the British what to do, but not whom to put in command. Only Churchill could fire Monty. Second, Ike realized that the politics of the Allied forces made it impossible to dismiss Montgomery, because Monty was the most popular general in the British Army. If Eisenhower had asked Churchill to relieve Montgomery there would have been an uproar in England and a serious loss of morale among the British troops in France. Ike could not get rid of Monty; he had to learn to bring out the best in the British general. It was a long, slow, painful process, but in the end Ike succeeded. It was one of his triumphs.

The first major flare-up came in mid-July, when Montgomery finally launched an attack against Caen. He told his subordinates that the objective was to kill Germans and pull Wehrmacht reinforcements on to Caen, so the American force could break out of Normandy. But he told Eisenhower something different—that he intended to break through at Caen and march on Paris, and, in pursuit of that goal, he wanted a tremendous air bombardment in the path of his advance. Eisenhower sent the bombers, which were badly needed elsewhere, and nearly 2,000 of them dropped over 7,000 tons of bombs in

157

Monty's path. But Monty called off his own attack after gaining seven miles. He announced that he was satisfied with the results.

Eisenhower thundered that it had taken more than seven thousand tons of bombs to gain seven miles and that the Allies could hardly hope to go through France paying a price of a thousand tons of bombs per mile. Tedder said Monty had failed and should be sacked; other British officers (and nearly every American) at SHAEF agreed. Tedder said he would take up the matter of Monty's dismissal with Churchill himself.

During this period, Ike relieved his frustrations by making frequent trips to France; his headquarters was still in England, while Montgomery had direct command of the land battle. During these visits Ike tried to see as many of his old friends as possible, check on how his division commanders were doing, chat with the foot soldiers, and in general see for himself how things were going.

At Normandy on July 3 Ike decided he wanted to do some driving. Sending his driver into the jeep's back seat, with only his British aide, James Gault, to accompany him, Ike set off on the tricky, narrow Normandy roads. At one point he managed to drive the jeep right through the front lines without being noticed, spent an hour behind German lines, and returned without incident. Indeed, Ike did not know he had been in any danger until he reached 90th Division headquarters and was told where he had been. The GI's were delighted to see him driving the jeep and shouted and whistled as he drove past.

The next day, July 4, while visiting a fighter airfield, he learned that a mission was about to be flown. Ike said he wanted to go along in order to see the country from the air. Bradley, who was with him, was against it, but Ike insisted. His parting words as he climbed into a Mustang fighter were, "All right, Brad, I am not going to fly to Berlin."

Ike enjoyed being with Americans for a few days, days in which he could forget the complexities of being an Allied Commander. But the visit had to end, and by July 5 he was back in England, where he once again found himself hoping that Monty would get moving. Monty, however, stuck to his plan, though he still continued to tell Eisenhower that he intended to break out at Caen. Tension rose at SHAEF, but just as things began to reach a crisis, Montgomery's plan paid off. The Germans had concentrated on his front line, which allowed Bradley and the Americans on his right to break through the enemy defenses. As the Americans dashed off toward Paris, the Germans facing Montgomery had to pull back, so Montgomery's troops began advancing too. Eisenhower now had what he wanted—a general advance all along his front.

And what an advance it was! The Allies roared through France, driving the Wehrmacht before them like so many sheep. What had once been the best army in Europe was now a thoroughly defeated shell of its former self. Much of the credit properly belongs to Montgomery, who gleefully sent his troops on the heels of the retreating Germans, covering scores of miles each day, taking thousands of prisoners, picking up hundreds of abandoned tanks and trucks and artillery pieces, and pushing right up to the German border. By August 25 Paris had been liberated; by early September the Allies had driven the Germans from France.

The liberation of Paris was one of the grand scenes of the war. The famous city had been held in gray bondage to the Nazis for four years; it needed a celebration. On August 26, after relighting the flame at the Tomb of the Unknown Soldier, de Gaulle led a parade down the Champs Elysées. Nearly two million people were there, on the streets, at the windows, on the roofs, hanging on flagpoles and lampposts. De Gaulle marched. Finally he stopped, turned, looked at the crowd, drew himself up to his full height, and in a hoarse, off-key voice, with his tears soaking the sacred soil of France, began to sing "La Marseillaise."

Eisenhower and Bradley decided to visit the city the next morning—since it would be a Sunday, Ike assured Bradley that "everyone will be sleeping late. We can do it without any fuss."

Sunday was a beautiful, sunny morning, so the weather added to the mood of gaiety and the happy feeling of liberation. No one slept late. Bicycles crowded the road. Cheering Parisians quickly recognized Ike and Bradley and surrounded them, holding up their fingers in the "V for Victory" sign, waving, and occasionally grabbing and kissing the generals. One huge Frenchman slathered Ike on both cheeks as the crowd shouted in delight.

Ike and Bradley called on de Gaulle at the Prefecture of Police. De Gaulle requested some show of Allied force

Paris was liberated on August 25, 1944. At the end of the war, searchlights flare a "V for Victory."

in order to establish his new authority and to cow any German troops left hidden in the city. Ike asked Bradley if anything could be done. Bradley said he was planning to attack eastward out of Paris and he could march his men straight through the city rather than around its outskirts. Ike decided to have two American divisions march through Paris on their way to battle. This not only gave de Gaulle his show, but it also reminded the Parisians

161

that their city had been liberated, as Ike put it, by "the grace of God and the strength of Allied arms." The parade became, in Ike's words, "possibly the only instance in history of troops marching in parade through the capital of a great country to participate in pitched battle on the same day."

On September 1, 1944, Eisenhower took personal command of the land battle. Until then Montgomery had been in charge, operating under Eisenhower's supervision but with considerable freedom of action. But as the numbers of American divisions in Europe increased, Eisenhower promoted Bradley to command of a group of armies, making him Monty's equal. Under the new arrangement, Monty commanded the 21st Army Group (a Canadian army and a British army) while Bradley commanded the 12th Army Group (two, later three, American armies, including one led by Patton). Now both Monty and Bradley reported to and took their orders from Eisenhower.

Eisenhower's assumption of direct command displeased Montgomery. The British general argued that Ike had too many responsibilities to pay enough attention to the day-by-day progress of the battle and should appoint someone to run the land war for him. Naturally, Monty thought he himself was the man for the job. Ike turned down innumerable requests from Monty for sole command and never lost his patience. But the issue continued to make their relations difficult.

Montgomery wanted sole command for reasons that went far beyond desire for fame or power. His view of how the battle should be fought was entirely different from Eisenhower's. After the liberation of Paris, Eisen-

162

hower ordered his armies to advance more or less abreast. Montgomery considered this wasteful. Monty wanted Ike to stop the American armies around Paris, then give all their supplies to his 21st Army Group, which in turn would make a concentrated attack, break through the German defenses along the Franco-German border, and dash on to Berlin. With the fall of Berlin the war in Europe would end.

Montgomery knew there was risk involved, but Britain was losing men and supplies every day at an alarming rate, and they could not be replaced. Unlike the Americans, whose homeland had not been touched and whose industrial strength was growing all the time, the British were at the end of their resources. Each day the war went on meant further losses, losses that could not be made up. Even though it was on the winning side in the war, Britain was rapidly losing its position as a great power.

The British desperately needed a quick end to the war so they could begin reconstructing their economy; the Americans could afford to take their time. Monty was willing to take a great risk in order to achieve a great end. Ike was less concerned with winning quickly than with making sure it was the Allies who won. It was a basic disagreement between two honest men; it could only be resolved by one giving in to the other.

This debate would become one of the hottest controversies of World War II. Eisenhower's approach was called "a broad-front advance," while Montgomery's alternative was called "the single thrust." Eisenhower's method was safe and sure, but it took time; Montgomery's proposal was risky but, if it worked, it promised a quick end to the war. The question of who was right can never be settled because Montgomery's way was never tried. We do know that Eisenhower's broadfront approach worked, but it is also true that the Allies did not win the war in 1944, even after their smashing victory in France. Had Monty's single thrust been tried, and had it worked, the Allies might have forced the Germans to surrender in October of 1944.

The key difficulty in pursuing Monty's strategy, as Ike saw it, was the lack of adequate port facilities. SHAEF had only the port of Cherbourg to draw upon for supplies, and Cherbourg was too small to handle the vast quantities of food, ammunition, tanks, trucks, and other materials the Allied armies required. If Monty were allowed to make a thrust for Berlin he would need all the supplies coming into Europe, which would mean that Bradley would have to stop and hold his armies in place. Thus all credit for the victory would have gone to the British 21st Army Group. Eisenhower was an Allied commander and he was not an extreme nationalist by any means, but he could never allow the Americans to stand by and watch the British get all the glory. Even had he been willing to do so, Roosevelt and Marshall—and the American people—would not have allowed it.

Aside from these political considerations, Eisenhower was convinced that the broad front was better than the single thrust. He was not at all sure he could get enough supplies to the 21st Army Group to carry it through to Berlin, even if he cut Bradley's supplies to a minimum; and he was afraid that once Monty broke through he would not be able to protect his exposed flank. It would not take the Germans long to figure out that Patton's tanks had no gasoline; the Wehrmacht would then concentrate all its strength against Monty and might possibly destroy the 21st Army Group. And, by this time, the Wehrmacht was showing signs of putting itself back together again.

A crisis came in October. Monty had tried to cross the Rhine River and move on into Germany, but his attempt failed, mainly because he did not have sufficient supplies to keep his armies moving. Montgomery said the trouble had been the American 12th Army Group, which had also kept up its offensive during that period and thus used up tons of supplies. The British general claimed that it was Ike's plans that had failed and the only thing to do now was to give him, Montgomery, command of Bradley's 12th Army Group.

One of Monty's many irritating characteristics was that he would never go to SHAEF headquarters to talk with Eisenhower—instead, the Supreme Commander had to go to Montgomery's headquarters to see him. Monty said this was necessary because all the people at SHAEF were his enemies and would gang up on him. So Ike, who had recently twisted his knee (the same knee he had hurt in football at West Point), flew to Brussels to see Montgomery. Eisenhower couldn't climb out of the airplane, so Monty came aboard for a conference. He began by demanding that Eisenhower's staff officers leave the plane, even though he had one of his own staff officers with him. Ike agreed. Monty then pulled Eisenhower's most recent orders from his pocket and damned Eisenhower's policy. Ike sat silent as the tirade mounted in

Monty was often impossible, but Ike had to handle him. The Britisher summed it up later: "I owe much to your wise guidance and kindly forbearance," he wrote Ike, "and I do not suppose I am an easy subordinate; I like to go my own way. But you have kept me on the rails in difficult and stormy times, and have taught me much." Monty thanked Ike and signed off, "Your very devoted friend, Monty."

fury. At the first pause for breath, however, Ike leaned forward, put his hand on Montgomery's knee, and said, "Steady, Monty! You can't speak to me like that. I'm your boss." Montgomery mumbled that he was sorry.

Montgomery then proposed that he make a single thrust to Berlin, but Ike refused even to consider the possibility. As Eisenhower put it in the office diary later, "Monty's suggestion is simple, give him everything, which is crazy."

Montgomery realized that he had lost, but he did not give up. A few days later he sent Ike a long letter, pointing out all the mistakes SHAEF had made during the campaign and voicing other complaints. He accused Eisenhower of allowing nationalistic prejudices to interfere with the proper running of the war and again demanded that he be given command of Bradley's armies.

Eisenhower had had enough. He sent a letter to Montgomery, telling him that under no circumstances would he receive sole battlefield command. Eisenhower said the campaign so far had been a huge success, not a failure as Monty charged, and even though it was true that the Allied advance had slowed down since reaching the German border, this was because of supply difficulties and increased Wehrmacht resistance, not faulty strategy. "It would be quite futile to deny that questions of nationalism often enter our problems," Eisenhower confessed. But he added, "It is nations that make war, and when they find themselves associated as Allies, it is quite often necessary to make concessions that recognize the existence of inescapable national differences. It is the job of soldiers to meet their military problems sanely, sensibly, and logically, and, while not shutting our eyes to the fact that

167

we are two different nations, produce solutions that permit effective cooperation, mutual support and effective results."

After delivering the lecture, Eisenhower made a threat. He said he was well aware of his own powers and limitations, "and if you, as the senior Commander in this Theater of one of the great Allies, feel that my conceptions and directives are such as to endanger the success of operations, it is our duty to refer the matter to higher authority for any action they may choose to take, however drastic." In other words, if Monty wanted to continue the argument, Eisenhower would tell the Combined Chiefs of Staff that his and Monty's differences could not be resolved and one of them must go. And both Ike and Monty knew that if the Chiefs had to pick between them, they would have to stick to Ike and fire Monty. This was not necessarily because Eisenhower was right and Montgomery wrong, but because three out of every four of the fighting men in Europe were Americans, and nearly all SHAEF's supplies came from America. Under those circumstances, the Supreme Commander had to be an American.

Monty gave in. "I have given you my views and you have given your answer," he replied to Eisenhower's letter. "I and all of us will weigh in one hundred percent to do what you want and we will pull it through without a doubt." He said he would carry out Ike's orders and promised, "You will hear no more on the subject of command from me." He signed off, "Your devoted and loyal subordinate."

Two months later Monty and other British officials, led

by Lord Alan Brooke and Churchill, again raised the question of a single thrust, which remained a subject for dispute almost until the day the Germans surrendered. The story of these controversies is long and complex; what stood out was that Eisenhower continued to make the decisions and enforce his will. He had to stand up against heavy pressure, including frequent personal visits and messages from Churchill. He managed to do so because of his own self-confidence. He was sure that he had taken everything into account, gathered all important information, and considered all possible alternatives. Then he acted. This is the essence of command.

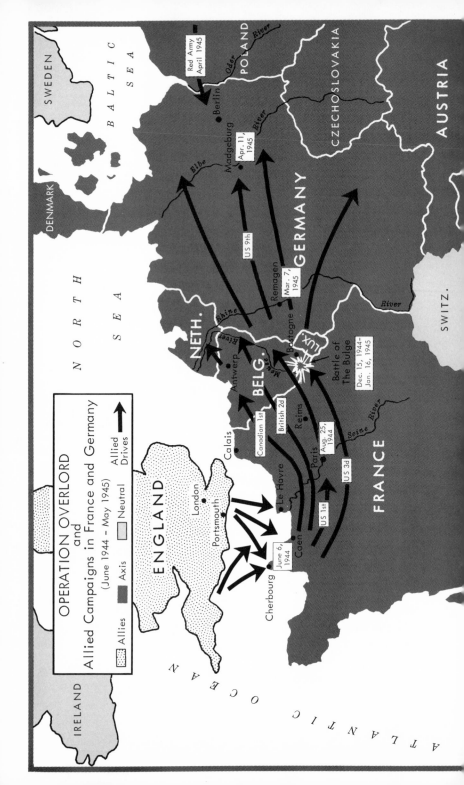

OPERATION OVERLORD
and
Allied Campaigns in France and Germany
(June 1944 – May 1945)

Allies
Neutral
Axis
Allied Drives

IRELAND

ENGLAND
London
Portsmouth

NORTH SEA

SWEDEN

DENMARK

BALTIC SEA

Calais

Le Havre
Cherbourg
Caen
June 6, 1944

NETH.
Antwerp
BELG.
Bastogne
LUX.

Battle of The Bulge
Dec. 15, 1944–
Jan. 16, 1945

Canadian 1st
British 2d
Reims
Paris
Aug. 25, 1944
US 1st
US 3d

Rhine River
Meuse River
Seine River

River

Remagen
Mar. 7, 1945

Elbe

Madgeburg
Apr. 11, 1945

Berlin

Red Army
April 1945

Oder River

POLAND

GERMANY

US 9th

CZECHOSLOVAKIA

AUSTRIA

SWITZ.

FRANCE

ATLANTIC OCEAN

chapter twelve
The Battle of the Bulge

A major reason for the argument between Eisenhower and Montgomery was the lack of progress on the battlefield. After driving the Germans from France, the Allies ran up against prepared German defensive positions along the German border at just the moment when their own supply situation was at its worst. SHAEF's armies advanced nearly three hundred miles during September, 1944, but for the remainder of the year they made almost no gains. At the beginning of October it had appeared certain that the Germans would surrender before Christmas; by the end of October it was clear that the Allied forces would not even get inside Germany, much less to Berlin, before spring, 1945. After the great victories of September, everyone in the Allied camp suffered a letdown. Tempers were short, staff officers snapped at one another, senior commanders blamed each other for the failure to finish the war.

The cause of the temporary stalemate lay, however, not in the Allied camp but with the Wehrmacht. In what the Germans called "the Miracle of the West" they had managed to put their divisions back together, scrape up some reserves, restore morale, and recover from the defeat in France. And they were now fighting on their own soil, which helped enormously. As Eisenhower told Roosevelt, "People of the strength and war-like tendencies of the Germans do not give in; they must be beaten to the ground."

In pursuit of that goal, Eisenhower ordered a general offensive. He wanted to keep the pressure on the Germans, eliminate as many Wehrmacht troops as possible, and improve his position so that when spring came he could leap across the Rhine River and overrun Germany. He had settled down to a war of attrition; his strategy was similar to General Grant's in the American Civil War. When Grant took command of the Union armies in 1864 he recognized that the Confederates would never surrender as long as they could maintain an army in the field. There was no shortcut to victory. But Grant could replace his losses, while the Confederates could not make up theirs. Thus his strategy was a simple one—force the Confederates to fight until they had no men left. Then the war would end. Like Grant, Eisenhower justified what many experts regarded as a cautious, cold-blooded strategy on the grounds that in the long run "this policy would result in shortening the war and therefore in the saving of thousands of Allied lives."

The people who pay the price for a war of attrition are the front-line soldiers. The 1944 fall campaign in Europe was the least glamorous, and the hardest, of the entire war. The Allied enlisted men fought against bitter opposition, with rain and snow adding to the difficulties of mines, artillery, and the German infantry. Gains were measured in yards, or rather in numbers of Germans killed. It was war at its worst.

Ike spent much of his time visiting the troops. He tried to see every division under his command, talk with as many men as possible, and spend at least some time with the officers. The trips involved a great deal more than simply showing himself to the front-line troops, for Ike picked up much valuable information during his visits—and not incidentally he greatly enjoyed being at or near the front lines, where he could see what was really happening.

While on a trip in November, for example, he noticed that his rules on recreation, rest, and comfort for the enlisted men were not being applied. He sent a new set of orders around, telling his subordinates what he wanted done and emphasizing that the major problem was "equality of treatment as between officers and enlisted men." He pointed out that GI's had complained to him that officers had whiskey rations while enlisted men did not, that commanders disapproved leave for enlisted men but granted it freely to officers, that when units were out of the line the men had to stay in their tents while the officers had the use of a car, that on the voyage over to the Continent the GI's had been jammed into the ships' holds while the officers had ample deck space, and so on.

The Supreme Commander wanted all these conditions changed. He laid it down as an order that "care must be

Arthur Tedder (lighting his pipe at right) *was Ike's Deputy Supreme Commander, the highest ranking British officer at SHAEF.*

taken that privileges given to officers in any unit must be available in proper proportion to enlisted men." If, for example, a unit could provide a jeep or a car for its officers when out of the line, that vehicle should never be used for recreational trips unless the unit could provide a similar privilege to the enlisted men. Leave and furlough policies had to be applied with absolute fairness. All captured wine should be issued "on a basis where the

174

enlisted man receives exactly as much as any officer." (Ike hoped, rather optimistically, that captured whiskey would be reserved for medical use.) Finally, he ordered his division commanders to drive around their areas, unannounced, so that they could "find out for themselves what conditions actually are and take proper steps for correction of defects." Then, just in case anyone missed the principal point, Ike concluded, "Officers must invariably place the care and welfare of their men above their own comfort and convenience."

Eisenhower had a lot of troops to think about. His armies were stretched out over a wide front, from Holland in the north to the Swiss border in the south. By December he had four American, one British, one Canadian, and one French army under his command, but even a force of that size was not equally strong across the entire front. Because he wanted to continue the offensive and thus needed large forces in certain areas, Eisenhower's line was thin in other places.

In the Ardennes forest, for example, two divisions held a front that would ordinarily require ten divisions. Although the Germans had broken through the French lines at the Ardennes back in 1940, Eisenhower was not particularly worried about the situation there. The Ardennes was heavily wooded, broken country with few good roads. The Germans had pushed through in 1940 with their modern tanks, but Ike felt that now, in 1944, they did not have enough tanks or sufficient gasoline to try again.

He was wrong, badly wrong. In November, Hitler quietly transferred ten divisions from the Russian front. They hid in the Ardennes forest, waiting for preparations for a counteroffensive to be completed, and waiting also for bad weather. With the Allies in complete command of the air, the Germans could not move during the daylight hours when the sky was clear—German vehicles spotted on the road were targets for Allied fighters or bombers. When rain or snow came, however, the Allies would be unable to fly any missions, and thus would lose their one great advantage over the Germans.

Hitler's plan was to break through Eisenhower's line in the Ardennes, then push on westward toward the English Channel. His generals were opposed to this counteroffensive because they did not have enough gasoline available to go fifty miles, much less all the way to the objective, Antwerp. Hitler told them not to worry— once they broke through, the tank crews could capture American gasoline behind Eisenhower's lines and use it to get to Antwerp. Antwerp was now the major port for SHAEF, so its capture could be decisive. Without a steady flow of supplies, Eisenhower's armies would starve. Hitler could even dream of driving them into the sea and thereby winning the war. It was a bold plan. Hitler was taking great risks, but he realized that if he did not drive the Allies back during the winter of 1944, they would overrun Germany in the spring of 1945.

At dawn on December 16, 1944, two German panzer armies with a total of twenty-four divisions struck an American corps in the Ardennes. The attack was a complete surprise. Two American divisions were trampled and all along this front the Americans retreated in great confusion. German tank crews rolled forward singing and shouting gleefully, reminding each other of their 1940 rout of the French Army.

How had it happened? Eisenhower's intelligence officers were supposed to keep track of enemy troop dispositions and warn him of possible enemy moves, but they had failed to prepare him for this counteroffensive. But the fault, ultimately, was Eisenhower's alone, as he knew perfectly well; a week after the attack began he dictated a memorandum accepting full responsibility. He had failed to read the mind of the enemy commander correctly. He was the man responsible for the weakness of the line in Ardennes, the one who had insisted on continuing the offensives north and south of the forest region. Because of his insistence on a general offensive, SHAEF had no reserve troops available to stop the counterattack. Most of all, he had insisted on maintaining the offensive; Eisenhower and his subordinates had continued to think about what they could do to the Germans, not what the Germans might do to them. The result was a surprise, and any commander whose troops are surprised has not done his job.

But despite his mistakes Eisenhower was the first Allied general to grasp the full import of the attack, the first to be able to readjust his thinking, the first to realize that although the counteroffensive and the initial Allied losses were painful, Hitler had in fact given him a magnificent opportunity. Eisenhower had a total of four divisions out of the line of battle, unengaged. On the first day of the attack he sent one to the southern end of the Bulge, as the German penetration of the Allied line was called, and another to the northern end. Then, studying the map, he put his finger on Bastogne and called it the key point. Bastogne had an excellent road system, and without control of Bastogne the Germans would not be able to drive through the Ardennes toward Antwerp. Ike ordered the U.S. 101st Airborne Division to Bastogne and told the commander to hold at all costs. He then began to prepare his fourth available division, the U.S. 82nd Airborne, for a counterattack of his own. These were the crucial moves of what became the Battle of the Bulge.

On December 19 Eisenhower met the Allied high command in a cold, damp squad room in a Verdun barracks, with only a lone potbellied stove to ease the chill. It was snowing; the Germans had predicted the weather correctly and staged their offensive during a period of terrible winter storms. The Allied Air Force was grounded. The Germans were attacking Bastogne with three divisions, sending the rest forward toward the Meuse River. The situation was serious at best; all the senior generals at SHAEF looked glum.

Ike opened the meeting by declaring, "The present situation is to be regarded as one of opportunity for us and not of disaster. There will be only cheerful faces at this conference table." Patton quickly picked up the theme. "Hell, let's have the guts to let the sons of bitches go all the way to Paris," he said, grinning broadly. "Then we'll really cut 'em off and chew 'em up."

But brave words and grinning faces could not stop German panzers. Eisenhower pointed out that it was crucial to hold at Bastogne, then make sure the Germans did not get across the Meuse River, where they could capture the Allied gasoline supplies. Ike correctly assumed that the Germans' key weakness was a shortage of fuel and he rightly guessed that they counted on capturing Allied stocks. He told his commanders to do everything possible to prevent the Germans from getting that gasoline.

Holding at the Meuse was only one part of his plan, Ike explained. Equally important was his own counterattack. He was not going to let the Germans emerge from their defensive positions without punishing them. Ike told Patton to break off his offensive south of the Bulge, change directions, and organize a major counterblow against the German southern flank. Patton protested that he wanted to keep his current offensive going, but Eisenhower sharply commanded him to do as he was told.

Over the next few days Ike supervised the preparations for the counterattack and urged the paratroopers of the 101st at Bastogne to hold on. The Germans continued to move forward, but the rate of advance was slow because they could not use the roads leading into and out of Bastogne. The bad weather made it impossible for Eisenhower to air-drop supplies to the 101st, which was surrounded and short on ammunition, medical supplies, and food. To add to his difficulties, the Germans had organized a special group of English-speaking German soldiers, dressed them in captured American uniforms, given them American jeeps to drive, and spread them behind the American lines. Their mission was to issue false orders, spread panic, and capture bridges and road junctions. A rumor spread, however, that their main objective was to assassinate the Supreme Commander.

Everyone at SHAEF became extra security-conscious. Ike was sealed into his headquarters at the Trianon Palace outside Paris. Guards with machine guns were placed all around the Palace, and when Ike went to Verdun or elsewhere for a meeting he was surrounded by armed guards in jeeps. An aide insisted that he start wearing a pistol; he did so for a day and then threw it aside, muttering that it was all a lot of foolishness. One aide noted that Ike "is a prisoner of our security police and is thoroughly but helplessly irritated by the restriction on his moves." After two days of confinement, Ike came out of his office and grumbled, "Hell's fire, I'm going out for a walk. If anyone wants to shoot me, he can go right ahead. I've got to get out!" Slipping out a back door, he walked around the grounds in the deep snow until a military policeman forced him back inside.

Military policemen were everywhere. Understandably nervous at the idea of so many German soldiers running around in American uniforms, MP's stopped every passing car and, ignoring rank and credentials, quizzed the occupants on American slang and customs in an attempt to distinguish real GI's from English-speaking Germans. One favorite question was to identify Mickey Mouse. Baseball questions were popular. General Bradley was held for an hour by an MP who had asked him the name of the capital of Illinois. Bradley correctly replied that it was Springfield, but the MP thought it was Chicago and put him under arrest. Later Bradley had to identify the position of the guard in football and a movie star's husband. The effect of all the super-security was to produce panic, and it began to seem as if Ike had lost his nerve.

That impression grew stronger when Eisenhower gave Monty command of the American army north of the Bulge. Ike did it because Bradley's lines of communications and the telephone wires connecting him with the men on the northern flank had been cut. But to Monty it seemed that Eisenhower had finally accepted his argument about a single ground commander—even that Ike had thrown up his hands helplessly and needed Monty to save the day.

In fact, nothing of the sort had happened, but Montgomery believed what he wanted to believe. According to a British officer who was there, he strode into the headquarters of the American army put under his command "like Christ come to cleanse the temple." But while Monty scurried about acting as though he had come to rescue the Americans from their mistakes, Eisenhower continued to shape the battle. He moved reinforcements to the front and prepared for the counterattack. On December 21, in an order of the day sent to everyone under his command, Eisenhower said of the enemy, "We cannot be content with his mere repulse. By rushing out from his fixed defenses the enemy may give us the chance to turn his great gamble into his worst defeat. Let everyone hold before him a single thought—to destroy the enemy on the ground, in the air, everywhere—destroy him!"

Eisenhower's lack of reserve troops worried him, so he made an offer to military criminals who were under court-martial sentences. Any man who would pick up a rifle and go into the battle could have a pardon and a clean slate. Those who had fifteen years or more at hard labor ahead of them volunteered. Ike also offered black troops serving in segregated supply units a chance to join white infantry units.

When General Smith saw this offer he blew up. In a stern note to Ike he pointed out that such racial integration ran directly against War Department policy, which was to organize the Army on segregated lines. Smith also thought it would be disastrous to try to integrate Army units.

Eisenhower, hardly a social revolutionary, gave in. He withdrew the offer and rewrote it. The upshot was that the blacks who volunteered—and thousands did, including black noncommissioned officers who had to revert to the rank of private before they were allowed to serve in combat units—were segregated into all-black platoons, under orders from white noncoms and officers.

During this period Eisenhower had given standing orders to the commander of the 101st Airborne Division, General Tony McAuliffe. The order read, "Hold Bastogne." Despite intensive fire from three and sometimes more German divisions, the 101st stayed. The paratroopers caught the imagination of the press, which took to calling them "the battered bastards of Bastogne." The men were short of all supplies; the Germans launched fierce attacks; the weather was bitterly cold. The attacks reached their peak on December 22. At noon on that day the Germans issued an ultimatum calling for "the honorable surrender of the encircled town." McAuliffe sent back a one-word answer: "Nuts."

The following day the weather broke and Eisenhower got every plane in SHAEF into the air. Big transports air-dropped supplies to the 101st, while fighters and bombers tore into the German lines, hitting them with fragmentation bombs, napalm, and machine-gun fire. The German offensive had been stopped. The question now was whether or not the Allies could annihilate the exposed German troops.

On December 26 Eisenhower met with his assistants in

the Trianon. Bending over a huge map, Ike pointed and declared, "I'll tell you, boys, what should be done." He wanted Patton on the south and Monty on the north to begin the counterattack as soon as possible.

Unfortunately, Monty was not ready. Worse, he had rubbed salt into the wound created when Ike gave him command of the American armies north of the Bulge (an action that Bradley and other Americans had regarded as an insult) by saying that if his plan for a single thrust had been followed none of this would have happened. "Now we are in a proper muddle," Monty told Bradley, but added that the future looked bright because the GI's were great fighting men when given proper leadership— meaning, of course, his own. None of this made cooperation between Bradley and Patton on the one hand, and Monty on the other, any easier.

These difficulties were multiplied when Monty announced that the time for a counterattack had not come. He wanted to wait a week, bring more men to the front, and prepare for additional ammunition and fuel reserves. That the delay ran directly counter to the Supreme Commander's clear orders bothered Montgomery not at all; he remained determined to save the Americans from their own follies.

As at Caen, however, he was willing to mislead Eisenhower. On December 27 he sent word that he had a plan for an attack. "Praise God from whom all blessings flow," Ike remarked, but added that he was flying to see Monty the next day to make sure the attack got started. At the meeting he learned that Monty disagreed with him on the situation; the British general thought the Germans had enough strength left for one more attack, so he wanted to keep his troops in reserve until it came. Eisenhower said that was nonsense; what he feared was not another attack but an escape—the Germans could pull out of the Bulge and retreat to their prepared defensive system. Ike insisted, "We must not allow that to happen." Still Monty hesitated. They finally agreed to wait until January 1. If the Germans had not attacked by then, Monty would strike on that date—or at least that is what Eisenhower thought Monty agreed to do.

But on December 30 Freddie De Guingand, Montgomery's Chief of Staff, came to SHAEF headquarters with the bad news that Monty would not attack until January 3. "What makes me so goddamn mad," Eisenhower's Chief of Staff remarked, "is that Monty won't talk in the presence of anyone else." In his place Monty had sent De Guingand. And now De Guingand repeated Montgomery's demand that he be given sole command of the land battle.

Eisenhower was furious. The Supreme Commander had a legendary temper, but it was shown only to his closest associates. When he was angry he worked off his tension by tearing a cloth handkerchief into tiny pieces, holding it under his desk as he did, so that no one knew how upset he was. Eisenhower went through three handkerchiefs that day. He had kept his temper with Monty as long as he could, because of the great importance of holding the Alliance together. Ike had hesitated to get tough because he feared it would have a bad effect on the Alliance, but now he was too upset to go easy.

In De Guingand's presence, Ike dictated a blistering

letter to Monty, demanding that he live up to his promises. If he did not, Ike threatened to ask Churchill to sack him. De Guingand begged Ike not to send the letter for twenty-four hours, so that he could see Monty and explain to him how serious the situation was. Ike reluctantly agreed.

De Guingand had a hard time convincing Monty that his job was at stake, but the British general finally realized that he had gone too far. He sent a note to Ike promising to carry out orders in the future. "You can rely on me and all under my command to go all out one hundred percent to implement your plan." He began his attack on January 2; Patton was already battering away at the German lines. During the next month the Allies kept attacking. Monty's slowness had lost them their best chance, but they did drive the Germans back into their original lines and in the process destroyed most of the German tanks. Ike had hoped for better results, but by mid-February, 1945, the enemy had lost its mobility and thus any possibility of maintaining a strong defense of Germany. Once the SHAEF forces broke through the German lines—which Eisenhower planned to do when spring and good weather arrived—the Allies would be able to dash through Germany at will. In that dash their commanding general would be Eisenhower, who had now firmly established himself as the man with the power.

chapter thirteen

The Last Decision: Berlin

With the defeat of the Germans at the Battle of the Bulge, Allied victory was in sight. The Red Army was closing in on Berlin from the east, while the Western Allies were pushing westward to the Rhine River. Between them they had the Wehrmacht caught in a vise, which they were slowly tightening. The Russians continued to do the bulk of the fighting—the Germans kept up to three hundred divisions in action against the Red Army, leaving only fifty or so to oppose the SHAEF units. In the air, meanwhile, British and American bombers were destroying the German industrial plant, especially in the Ruhr River region, where most German industry was located. Bombers and fighter planes continued to destroy German bridges, railroads, and highways, making it impossible for Wehrmacht units to move during the day. The final defeat of Hitler's Germany was only a question of time.

Imminent victory created some new problems for the

Allies. Every alliance in history has been formed for a special purpose, usually the defeat of a common enemy, as in the British-American-Russian alliance of World War II. And every alliance in history has broken up once victory was achieved. The reasons for this are easily understood—in the nature of things two countries cannot have similar long-range objectives. Once Hitler was eliminated, there would be little to hold the alliance together. The major British concern for the postwar world was colonialism—to preserve the British Empire. But Roosevelt was opposed to colonialism. The United States wanted a secure Europe built around a revived, non-Nazi Germany. But the British, French, and Russians were all afraid of the Germans and were opposed to restoring the country, much less allowing it to rebuild its destroyed industry. The Russians were mainly concerned with their own security against German attack and with spreading Communism throughout Europe. The latter interest was regarded by the Americans and British with horror.

There were scores of additional difficulties. Roosevelt wanted to hold the Grand Alliance together, primarily through the device of the United Nations, which was just being formed. He thought it important for America to make every effort to get along with the Russians, for in his view postwar cooperation between the United States and Russia was essential to world peace. Churchill, however, believed that once Hitler had been defeated there was no basis for British-American cooperation with Russia; he was more concerned with building the strength of the Western Allies in central Europe as a buffer against Communism than he was in getting along with Stalin.

*Even before Germany's defeat, Churchill, Roosevelt and Stalin
had carved it up at Yalta in February, 1945. The Big Three
divided Germany into occupation zones, and Berlin—which
would be inside the Russian zone—was cut into four sectors,
one for each of the Allies. This political decision was made long
before Ike faced the issue of which nation's army should be
raced ahead to Berlin.*

There was also the question of glory. Each member of the Big Three felt that it had made the major contribution to the war effort and ought to receive the credit for the final triumph. Each could make a good argument: the Russians had defeated the bulk of the German army; the British had fought alone against Hitler in 1940–41; the United States, through Lend-Lease, had supplied much of the military material for the other partners in the Alliance. The truth was that all three nations were essential to the victory; none could have done it alone or even in an alliance with only one other nation. Yet each nation wanted the sole credit for victory. In the last days of the war, this came down to one thing—each wanted its army to be the first to take the Nazi capital, Berlin.

The desire of all three nations to be the first into Berlin brought about some of Eisenhower's most difficult moments in the war. He had to decide, first, whether or not to race his forces against the Red Army to Berlin, and second, if he did start a race for the German capital, whether to send British or American divisions. Whatever he did would make two nations unhappy.

Ike was in a special position. As commander of an Allied force, he could not afford to make his decisions on nationalistic grounds; he had to decide what would be good for the Alliance as a whole. Patton wanted Ike to hold Montgomery's forces on the Rhine and give him their supplies, and then Patton could dash on to Berlin. Monty wanted Patton stopped where he was, with all Patton's supplies sent to *him*, and then Montgomery would send the British into Berlin. Churchill hoped that British troops would take the city, but he was mostly concerned with getting western troops there before the Russians. Roosevelt was opposed to any race for Berlin—in his view the Red Army should not be cheated out of the final triumph it had done the most to bring about. Thus Eisenhower's superiors as well as his subordinates were split over what he should do, but he was the only one who could make the final decision.

Command arrangements presented another difficulty. Churchill again raised the question of a single ground commander and suggested Montgomery. The British newspapers picked up the demand. When Bradley read a story to the effect that Montgomery should be given command over the American forces in Europe, he called on Ike and demanded to know how the Supreme Commander intended to respond. Ike impatiently indicated that he had no intention of doing anything about it, but Bradley was not satisfied with that quick reply. "You must know," Bradley declared, "after what has happened I cannot serve under Montgomery. If he is to be put in command of all ground forces, you must send me home, for if Montgomery goes in over me, I will have lost the confidence of my command."

Ike sat up. "Well," he said to Bradley, "I thought you were the one person I could count on for doing anything I asked you to." Bradley would not be put off. "You can, Ike," he replied. "I've enjoyed every bit of my service with you. But this is one thing I cannot take." He insisted that he would ask to be sent home rather than subordinate himself to Monty's command. So Eisenhower undertook his last campaign with his two most important subordinates nearly at each other's throats. But even that was a relatively minor difficulty. His greatest problem remained in picking the direction of his final advance.

After much thought, Eisenhower decided to leave Berlin to the Red Army and instead directed his forces toward what was left of the German Army. His decision has become the most controversial of the war. Ike's critics charge that he did not understand international politics—that by leaving Berlin to the Russians he lost the best chance the West had to prevent Communist control of Berlin and the surrounding territory of East Germany. The critics believe that had Eisenhower taken Berlin, the Russians could have been kept out of the city and their postwar territorial gains in Eastern Europe prevented.

The critics are badly mistaken, their charges absurd. There was never the slightest chance that the Russians could have been forced out of eastern Europe, which the Red Army (far larger than the combined British-American armies in Europe) had liberated while the Western Allies were still on the west bank of the Rhine River in extreme western Germany. Nothing could have driven the Russians out of territory they had already conquered. Beyond that, the division of Germany into occupation zones had already been made by political advisers to Stalin, Roosevelt, and Churchill. No matter who captured Berlin, the politicians had already agreed to split it into sectors, with each nation getting a part of the city. After taking Berlin, the Russians lived up to that agreement, and shortly after the war the British and Americans took their sectors of the city. There is no reason to believe that if the Western Allies had captured Berlin they would have gone back on their word and kept the Russians out. In short, in terms of the politics of the postwar world, it made no difference who captured Berlin.

Now, however, for purposes of honor and prestige, it did make a difference. Churchill told Ike: "I deem it highly important that we should shake hands with the Russians as far to the east as possible." He feared that otherwise the Russians' view that they had made the major contribution to the victory would be strengthened. What he mainly wanted, however, was glory for the British Army; as one of Ike's British officers at SHAEF put it, "Monty wanted to ride into Berlin on a white charger" and thus emerge as the hero of the war.

Throughout March and the first week of April, 1945, Ike planned to make his major thrust into Germany on the northern sector, under Montgomery's command. Patton could advance in the south with smaller forces. But these plans underwent a drastic change.

On March 7 Eisenhower was at his main headquarters at Reims, where he spent the day catching up on his work. After reviewing all the reports and attending a conference in the War Room, he dictated some personal letters to friends in the States. That evening he planned to relax and asked a few of his corps commanders to dinner. They had just sat down to eat when the telephone rang. Bradley wanted to talk to Eisenhower.

Bradley had been with General Harold "Pinky" Bull, Eisenhower's senior operations officer, when he learned of the lucky capture of an intact bridge over the Rhine River at Remagen in central Germany. "Hot dog," Bradley had shouted, and told his subordinates to get as many supplies and men across the Rhine as possible. Turning to Bull, Bradley laughed and declared, "There goes your ball game, Pink. We've gotten across the Rhine on a bridge." Now, Bradley felt, Ike would have to put the main force of the last offensive under his command in central Germany.

Bull shrugged and said that did not make any difference, because nobody was going anywhere from Remagen. "It just doesn't fit into *the* plan," Bull explained to Bradley. "Ike's heart is in your sector, but right now his mind is up north."

Bradley would not be put off. He could not believe that Ike was so rigid that he would ignore a bridgehead over the Rhine, even though it did not fit into previous plans and was in an area poorly suited to offensive operations. Bradley decided to call the Supreme Commander on the telephone.

Ike left the dining room to go into an adjacent office to take the call. Bradley told him about the bridge at Remagen. "Brad, that's wonderful," Ike exclaimed. Bradley said he wanted to push all the force he had in the vicinity over to the east bank of the Rhine. "Sure," Eisenhower responded. "Get right on across with everything you've got. It's the best break we've had."

Bradley, grinning at Bull, then told Eisenhower that the SHAEF operations officer opposed such a move because Remagen did not fit into the overall plan. "To hell with the planners," Ike replied. "Sure, go on, Brad, and I'll give you everything we got to hold that bridgehead. We'll make good use of it even if the terrain isn't too good."

And at that moment, Eisenhower changed his plans. Rather than making his major thrust into Germany under Montgomery in the north, he decided to take advantage of Remagen and make the thrust in the center, under Bradley. This reinforced his decision to ignore Berlin, for Bradley's objectives remained far south of the city.

In early April, 1945, when the Allied armies were across the Rhine River and sweeping through Germany, Churchill again put extreme pressure on Ike to concentrate behind Montgomery and drive to Berlin. Eisenhower replied that it made no military sense to strike out for Berlin, for "Berlin itself is no longer a particularly important objective. Its usefulness to the German has been largely destroyed and even his government is preparing to move to another area." There were few German units in and around Berlin, and the Red Army could take care of them. Moreover, Ike realized what no one else seemed to, namely, that by concentrating on destroying the Wehrmacht rather than on getting to Berlin first or on keeping the Russians out of central Europe, he could hold the Alliance together, at least until Hitler's defeat was complete. While everyone around him argued for his own nation's aims, Eisenhower stuck to the Alliance goal.

Ike was always clear about his aims. His orders from the Combined Chiefs were to defeat Germany—not to stop the Russian advance or to make sure Monty got to Berlin. "I am the first to admit that a war is waged in pursuance of political aims," Ike told Churchill, "and if the Combined Chiefs of Staff should decide that the Allied effort to take Berlin outweighs purely military considerations in this theater, I would cheerfully

An impressive sight, with his jutting chin, round shoulders, fat cigar, Churchill argued endlessly with Ike. Still, the two men respected and loved each other. Ike later paid tribute: "In countless ways he could have made my task a harder one had he been anything but big, and I shall always owe him an immeasurable debt of gratitude for his unfailing courtesy and zealous support, regardless of his dislike of some important decisions."

readjust my plans and my thinking so as to carry out such an operation." Thus, if Churchill was prepared to declare Russia the enemy instead of Germany and could get Roosevelt to agree, Eisenhower would willingly change his plans, for then the military considerations would be much different. But the Combined Chiefs did not change Ike's orders and the final decision stayed in his hands. Germany remained the enemy; Russia continued to be an ally.

None of this kept the British from criticizing. Given the stakes, they could not refrain. But neither could they expect Ike to hold his temper forever. In early April, after receiving a series of cables from the British questioning his policy, Ike blew up. The specific issues were familiar: the British wanted Ike to give top priority to Montgomery in northern Germany, and they wanted Monty sent toward Berlin. The man who did most of the criticizing was the Chief of the Imperial General Staff, Alan Brooke.

Ike expressed his feelings in a long letter to Marshall. After rejecting Brooke's suggestions, Ike declared, "Merely following the principle that Field Marshal Brooke has always shouted to me, I am determined to concentrate on one major thrust [in the center, under Bradley] and all that my plan does is to place the Ninth U.S. Army back under Bradley." As for Berlin, Ike said again that the city had no military importance.

In his conclusion, Ike allowed some of his frustrations to emerge. The Prime Minister and his Chiefs of Staff, he said, opposed most of SHAEF's strategic plans—"they opposed my idea that the German should be destroyed west of the Rhine before we made our major effort across that river. . . . Now they apparently want me to turn aside on operations in which would be involved many thousands of troops before the German forces are fully defeated. I submit that these things are studied daily and hourly by me and my advisors and that we are animated by one single thought which is the early winning of this war."

Churchill continued to push. When Ike insisted again that the major thrust would be under Bradley, Churchill complained about the minor role assigned the British. Churchill's message, according to the SHAEF office diary, "upset Eisenhower quite a bit." He dictated an immediate reply. "I am disturbed, if not hurt," Ike declared, "that you should suggest any thought on my part to 'relegate His Majesty's Forces to an unexpected restricted sphere.' Nothing is further from my mind and I think my record over two and a half years of commanding Allied forces should eliminate any such idea."

Eisenhower was not being totally candid with Churchill, a reflection perhaps of his irritation at having his every move called into question. He felt he had proven he should be trusted. Probably more important was the fact that he would not give in. Marshall had informed him that the American Chiefs of Staff were backing him, and Ike knew how strong his position was. He did not want to hurt or disturb the British, but neither would he allow them to set the objectives of his last campaign. Determined to hold to his own plan and launch his major offensive under Bradley, he still hoped to satisfy the British. Thus he refused to take up a discussion on Berlin with Churchill, which could only lead to bad feelings, or to admit that he had made any change in plan. If he were forced, however, he would speak out. "So earnestly did I believe in the military soundness of what we were doing," Eisenhower said in his memoirs, "that my intimates on the staff knew I was prepared to make an issue of it." Meanwhile, however, he had a war to fight.

Throughout April, 1945, the Allied forces rolled forward. Superiority in quality of troops, mobility, air power, supplies, and morale was enormous. Commanders chose objectives that, more often than not, were reached and captured even before the time they had set. Regiments, companies, squads, sometimes even three men in a jeep, dashed on ahead, leaving their supply bases far behind, ignoring wide gaps on their flanks and enemy units in the rear, roaming far and wide with only sketchy knowledge of the enemy's positions—all the time certain that there was little or nothing the Germans could do about it. The German high command was, for all practical purposes, gone; even regimental commanders did not know where their troops were. Most German units were immobilized because of the lack of fuel. There was no real defense—the Allies swept everything before them.

Ike felt a deep sense of pride as he watched the Americans drive forward. He wanted Marshall, the man who built the army that was doing so well, to share that feeling. "If you could see your way clear to do it," he wrote Marshall on April 15, "I think you should make a visit here while we are still conducting a general offensive." Eisenhower was sure Marshall would be proud of the army he had produced. The U.S. air and ground forces were operating as a unit "all the way down the line from me to the lowest private." Ike was sure that no organization had ever existed that could reshuffle and regroup on a large scale as well as the American Army in Europe could. This, in turn, was a reflection of the "high average of ability in our higher command team." Ike concluded with another plea to Marshall to come to Germany so he could see, "in visible form, the fruits of much of your work over the past five years." Eisenhower did not need to add that this would be Marshall's last opportunity to see the greatest armed force the United States had ever put together, for preparations were already under way to send parts of that army to the Pacific to finish the war against Japan. Unfortunately Franklin Roosevelt's death in mid-April prevented Marshall from making the trip.

The Allied armies, meanwhile, had spread out in all directions. Its dispersion soon became so great that army commanders did not know where their divisions were at any particular time of the day. Under the circumstances, Ike played a small role in the actual direction of the battle. He intervened only when a major change in the direction of an army movement was called for, or when a command question with political overtones was involved.

On April 11, 1945, spearheads of General William Simpson's Ninth Army reached the Elbe River at Magdeburg. Simpson got two bridgeheads over the Elbe; one was wiped out by a German counterattack on April 14, but the other held.

Suddenly it seemed that the Americans had an opportunity to take Berlin after all, even though the Allied armies were scattered across western Germany. The Russian drive for Berlin had not yet started—and Simpson was within fifty miles of the city. He thought he could get to Berlin before the Russians and he asked Bradley's permission to try.

Bradley checked with Eisenhower, who wanted to know Bradley's estimate of the cost of taking Berlin. About 100,000 casualties, Bradley replied, and commented, "A pretty stiff price to pay for a prestige objective."

With that dire forecast in mind, Eisenhower studied the map. Simpson was only fifty miles from Berlin and facing a weak German army, but he had just one small bridgehead, and a number of small rivers and streams stood between him and Berlin. At most Simpson could start 50,000 men for Berlin, with little artillery support. Ike had no troops immediately available to reinforce Simpson. On the other hand, the Red Army was only thirty-five miles from Berlin, had two solid bridgeheads over the Oder River, and was just beginning its offensive. The Russians were sending 1,250,000 men, with 22,000 pieces of artillery, toward Berlin. They were faced by two weak German armies and had flat, dry land between them and Berlin. As far as Ike could see, there was no way for Simpson to get to Berlin before the Russians. He told Simpson to drive south, toward the German forces near Austria, rather than east toward Berlin. The British, especially Churchill, were furious, but Eisenhower stuck to his position.

(After the war, when Russian actions in East Germany and their blockade of Berlin angered thousands of American citizens, criticism of Eisenhower mounted to a new fury. Again critics charged that he did not understand politics and should have taken Berlin in order to keep the Russians out. They assumed that capture of Berlin by the Americans would have made a great difference in the Cold War.

Ike was plagued with this charge throughout his political career. Seven years later, during his first campaign for the Presidency, he pointed out to a Denver audience that there never was any possibility of getting to Berlin ahead of the Russians. Then he reminded his audience that "none of these brave men of 1952 have yet offered to go out and pick the 100,000 American mothers whose sons should have made the sacrifice to capture a worthless objective.")

In late April the Russians battered their way into Berlin. Hitler personally directed the defense of the city; the Germans fought like madmen. The Russians lost at least 100,000 men but they gained the first somber sense of triumph, the first awesome sight of the ruins, the first parades under the pall of smoke. Two months later they gave to the West two thirds of the city they had captured at such an enormous price. At the cost of not a single life, both Great Britain and the United States had their sectors in Berlin. They have been there ever since.

On the Berlin question, Eisenhower had won, but that was not the most significant result of the long and often bitter debate. Given the difference in the size of the land forces Britain and America were contributing to the battle in Europe, Marshall's attitude, Ike's support from the British members of SHAEF, and Roosevelt's inclination to follow Marshall's lead in military matters, it was

Walter Smith (across the table, with other Allied chiefs) *represents Ike at the German surrender at Reims on May 7, 1945. German Chief of Staff Gustaf Jodl* (center, back to camera) *signs the document under which the battered Wehrmacht will lay down all arms in unconditional surrender. The war in Europe is over.*

inevitable that Eisenhower would have his way. His real achievement was that he had won without alienating the British. They felt strongly about the issues, and pressed their points as hard as they dared, giving Ike's patience a thorough testing. He kept turning them down, but only after giving them the opportunity to fully state their views, and he never let himself be provoked into losing his temper. At the end of the war—the Germans surrendered unconditionally on May 8, 1945—his reputation with the British remained extraordinarily high, a unique achievement for an Allied commander.

Monty summed up Eisenhower's achievement in a letter he wrote the Supreme Commander immediately after the surrender. "Dear Ike," he began, ". . . I suppose we shall soon begin to run our own affairs." Before the combined forces split up to occupy their separate zones in Germany, Monty wanted to say "what a privilege and an honor it has been to serve under you. I owe much to your wise guidance and kindly forbearance," he conceded. Montgomery said he knew his own faults very well—"I do not suppose I am an easy subordinate; I like to go my own way. But you have kept me on the rails in difficult and stormy times, and have taught me much." Montgomery thanked Eisenhower for all he had done for him and signed off, "Your very devoted friend, Monty."

Montgomery meant what he said. One of Eisenhower's remarkable achievements had been his ability to carry on long and complex arguments with the British without causing any personal offense. Beyond that, as Ike pointed out in his famous Guildhall Address of June 12, 1945, when he was being honored by the city of London, much had been achieved. When SHAEF was first formed there were many who feared that the British and Americans "could never combine together in an efficient fashion to solve the complex problems presented by modern war. I hope you believe we proved the doubters wrong. And, moreover, I hold that we proved this point not only for war—we proved it can always be done by our two peoples, provided only that both show the same good will, the same forbearance, the same objective attitude that the British and Americans so amply demonstrated in the nearly three years of bitter campaigning."

It was indeed a grand achievement, but Ike would never have dreamed of taking personal credit for it. As he said at Guildhall, "No man alone could have brought about this result. Had I possessed the military skill of a Marlborough, the wisdom of Solomon, the understanding of Lincoln, I still would have been helpless without the loyalty, vision, and generosity of thousands upon thousands of British and Americans."

Eisenhower concluded, "My most cherished hope is that . . . neither my country nor yours need ever again summon its sons and daughters from their peaceful pursuits to face the tragedies of battle. But—a fact important for both of us to remember—neither London nor Abilene, sisters under the skin, will sell her birthright for physical safety, her liberty for mere existence."

One final word must be said about Eisenhower in World War II. When associates (superiors or subordinates) described him, there was one word almost all of them used. It was "trust." From Churchill to the lowest British soldier, from Roosevelt to the buck private in the

*General of the Armies Dwight David Eisenhower with his troops
in Belgium in 1945.*

United States Army, from de Gaulle to the anonymous French Resistance fighter in southern France, people trusted Eisenhower.

They did so for the most obvious reason—he was trustworthy. His broad grin, his mannerisms, his approach to life, all illustrated his honesty. Montgomery never thought much of Eisenhower as a soldier; he once declared that "I would not class Ike as a great soldier in the true sense of the word." But he did appreciate other qualities. While he thought Eisenhower intelligent, "his real strength lies in his human qualities. He has the power of drawing the hearts of men towards him as a magnet attracts the bit of metal. He merely has to smile at you, and you trust him at once."

With his superiors and with foreign governments, with his staff and with his troops, Eisenhower did what he said he was going to do. His reward was the trust they placed in him. And because he was trusted, he was successful.

further reading

The best place to begin a study of Eisenhower's career is with his own writings. *At Ease: Stories I Tell to Friends* is an informal memoir, delightful to read, full of revealing incidents and anecdotes. *Crusade in Europe* is Eisenhower's own account of the campaigns of World War II; one of the best-selling books of the late 1940s and early 1950s, it has been called the finest memoir by a professional soldier since U. S. Grant. *Mandate for Change* and *Waging Peace* are Eisenhower's accounts of his years as President.

The fullest account of Ike's childhood and early years is *Soldier of Democracy* by Kenneth S. Davis; it's a marvelous book. The first work to consult for an understanding of the Army in which Ike served is Russell F. Weigley's *History of the United States Army*. *The Years of MacArthur* by D. Clayton James is an outstanding biography of the man under whom Eisenhower worked

207

during most of the 1930s. Interested students should also look at MacArthur's own *Reminiscences*.

Most of the famous soldiers of World War II wrote their memoirs. The most important memoirs for understanding Eisenhower's military career include Omar Bradley's *A Soldier's Story*, which is strongly pro-Eisenhower, and Arthur Bryant's *The Turn of the Tide* and *Triumph in the West*, which, like Bernard Montgomery's *Memoirs*, is extremely anti-Ike. For a more favorable British view of Eisenhower see Arthur Tedder's *With Prejudice*, and especially Winston Churchill's six-volume memoir, *The Second World War*.

George C. Marshall did not write his memoirs, but he gave extensive interviews to Forrest Pogue, who used them to write one of the great American biographies. Volume one, *Education of a General*, covers Marshall's life from 1899 to 1939; volume two, *Ordeal and Hope*, carries the story forward to 1943; volume three, *Organizer of Victory*, is concerned with the 1943–45 period. For an overall view of the American war effort, see *The Mighty Endeavor* by Charles MacDonald. The best one-volume history of the war is *History of the Second World War* by the British military historian B. H. Liddell Hart. For an inside view of Eisenhower, see *My Three Years with Eisenhower* by Harry Butcher, based on Butcher's diaries as Ike's aide.

By far the most important original source for understanding Eisenhower's role in the war is *The Papers of Dwight David Eisenhower: The War Years*, edited by Alfred D. Chandler, Jr., and myself. Here the student will find all the letters, orders, memoranda, and other papers Eisenhower wrote during the war, along with explanatory footnotes and text by the editors. I based my own book, *The Supreme Commander: The War Years of General Dwight D. Eisenhower*, on Eisenhower's papers. It is a thorough account of Ike's experiences.

Of the many criticisms of Eisenhower's decision not to go into Berlin the most important are *The Struggle for Europe*, by Chester Wilmot, *The Last Battle*, by Cornelius Ryan, and *The Last 100 Days*, by John Toland. All three authors agree that Ike could have taken Berlin before the Russians got there, that he should have done so, and that Allied occupation of Berlin would have made a great difference in the Cold War. For the opposite view, see my book *Eisenhower and Berlin: The Decision to Stop at the Elbe*.

S. E. A.
New Orleans, 1973

glossary

Afrika Korps—German Field Marshal Erwin Rommel's tank force, which fought Montgomery and Eisenhower in North Africa.

Allied Expeditionary Force—The combined British, American, and Canadian forces, land, sea, and air, that carried out the invasion of France and the campaign in Europe.

Allied Powers—The United States, Great Britain, and Russia.

Army—An army is composed of two or three corps, acting together (see *Corps* and *Division* below).

Axis Powers—Germany, Italy, and Japan.

BCOS—British Chiefs of Staff, composed of the head of each British armed service (air force, navy, army) plus Churchill's personal Chief of Staff.

Big Three—Churchill, Roosevelt, and Stalin; at times the term was used to indicate the nations they led: Britain, the U.S., and the U.S.S.R.

C&GS—Command and General Staff College at Leavenworth, Kansas; a U.S. Army postgraduate school.

CCS—Combined Chiefs of Staff, composed of the BCOS and the JCS acting together. The CCS was in overall command of the

Allied war effort, taking its orders directly from heads of state Churchill and Roosevelt.

Corps—A corps is composed of two or three divisions, acting together (see *Division* below).

Division—A division is the basic fighting unit of a modern army. It is self-contained; that is, it has its own artillery, airplane spotters, tanks, radio network, and so on, and thus is capable of fighting on its own. The size of a division varies enormously. In World War II the U.S. Army kept its divisions at about 12,000 men. The Wehrmacht and the Russian Red Army had some divisions with less than 5,000 men, although typically their divisions were closer to 10,000.

ETO—The U.S. Army's European Theater of Operations. In addition to his responsibilities as Allied Supreme Commander, Eisenhower was also in command of ETO—all American forces in and around northern Europe.

JCS—Joint Chiefs of Staff, the American counterpart of BCOS.

Luftwaffe—The German Air Force.

Overlord—Code name for the Allied invasion of France on June 6, 1944. The invasion is sometimes called "D-Day," but that phrase was applied to every amphibious operation of the war and meant only "the day the attack begins."

Panzer Division—A tank or armored division in the Wehrmacht.

Roundup—Code name for a proposed 1943 invasion of France. Not mounted.

SHAEF—Supreme Headquarters, Allied Expeditionary Force. SHAEF was a gigantic staff operation, directly responsible to Eisenhower or his Chief of Staff, Walter B. Smith.

Sledgehammer—Code name for a proposed 1942 invasion of France, to be carried out only if it appeared that the Russians were on the verge of surrender. Not mounted.

Torch—Code name for the November 8, 1942, invasion of French North Africa.

12th Army Group—Composed of the U.S. First, Third, and Ninth Armies, and commanded by General Omar Bradley.

21st Army Group—Composed of the British Second, the Canadian First, and at times the U.S. First and Ninth Armies, and commanded by General Bernard Montgomery.

Vichy Government—The government set up in Vichy, France, in 1940, after the armistice was signed between Germany and France. The Vichy government, headed by Marshal Pétain, collaborated with the Nazis and was opposed by Charles de Gaulle's Free France movement.

Wehrmacht—The German Army.

acknowledgments

Directly quoted material comes from the following:

AT EASE: STORIES I TELL TO FRIENDS, by Dwight D. Eisenhower (1967, Doubleday & Co., Inc.) Copyright © 1967 by Dwight D. Eisenhower.

CRUSADE IN EUROPE, by Dwight D. Eisenhower (1945, Doubleday & Co., Inc.) Copyright 1948 by Doubleday & Co., Inc.

THE PAPERS OF DWIGHT DAVID EISENHOWER: THE WAR YEARS, 5 vols., Alfred D. Chandler, Jr., and Stephen E. Ambrose, eds. (1970, The Johns Hopkins Press) Copyright © by The Johns Hopkins Press.

THE SUPREME COMMANDER: THE WAR YEARS OF GENERAL DWIGHT D. EISENHOWER, by Stephen E. Ambrose (1970, Doubleday & Co., Inc.) Copyright © 1969, 1970 by Stephen E. Ambrose.

Grateful thanks are due John Wickman and W. A. Scott of the Dwight D. Eisenhower Library in Abilene, Kansas, for their generosity in supplying many of the photographs in this book. Thanks are also due the United States Army and The Johns Hopkins University.

213

Picture credits:

index

Abilene (Kansas), 10–11
Adler, Cadet Corporal
    Thomas, 32, 33
Alexander, Gen. Harold,
    119–20, 121
Anderson, Gen. Kenneth,
    116, 117, 119, 120
Ardennes and Battle of the
    Bulge, 175–79, 182–86
Arnim, Gen. Jürgen von, 115,
    116, 119, 121

Badoglio, Pietro, 131–35
Baruch, Bernard, 64
Battle of the Bulge, 176–79,
    182–86
Berlin, push toward and cap-
    ture of, xiv, 163, 164,
    167, 171–73, 175, 185,
    186–87, 189–94, 196–
    201

Bonus Marchers (in Wash-
    ington, D.C.), 68–69,
    70
Bradley, Gen. Omar, 7, 38,
    119, 121, 122, 145–46,
    151, 153, 156, 159, 160–
    61, 162, 165, 180, 183,
    190, 192–93, 194, 196,
    197, 200
Brooke, Field Marshal Alan,
    169, 196
Bull, Gen. Harold ("Pinky),
    192–93

Churchill, Winston, xiv, 94,
    101–02, 104–05, 108,
    111, 112, 123, 132, 133,
    137, 141, 142, 145, 149,
    155, 157, 158, 169, 185,
    187, 189, 191, 192, 194,
    196, 197–98, 200

Connor, Gen. Fox, 54–55, 56, 57, 59, 71
Cunningham, Adm. Andrew, 113

Darlan, Adm. Jean-François, 110–14, 132
Davis, Bob, 20–21
de Gaulle, Charles, 108, 111, 112, 113, 125, 149, 160–61
De Guingand, Freddie, 184–85

Eisenhower, Arthur (brother), 12, 14, 15, 18, 122
Eisenhower, David (father), 13–18, 21, 23–27, 46
Eisenhower, Doud Dwight ("Icky"; son), 50, 52, 54
Eisenhower, Dwight David ("Ike")
birth, 12
childhood and early life, 12–21, 23–28
children—*see* Eisenhower, Doud Dwight, and Eisenhower, John
courtship and marriage to Mamie Geneva Doud, 41, 43–44, 45–46, 48
education, 20, 25, 26, 27, 31–38, 40
Guildhall Address, 203–04

Eisenhower, Dwight David (*cont'd*)
military career—*see below*
personal characteristics, xi, xii–xiii, xv, 19, 21, 38, 43, 46, 48, 53, 113, 137, 143–44, 155, 156, 184, 205–06
and political issues, xii–xvi, 42, 63, 67, 69, 109, 141
Eisenhower, Dwight David ("Ike")
military career, xiii, 41–43, 51–59, 75–78
in Philippines, 71–75
in Washington, 59–65, 67–71, 77–78
at West Point, 26, 27, 31–38, 40
World War I, 49–50, 50–51
World War II, xiii, xiv, xv, 80, 81–87, 90–102, 143, 168–69, 173, 175, 179–82, 203, 204, 206; Ardennes and Battle of the Bulge, 175–79, 182–86; Berlin, push toward and capture of, xiv, 164–65, 167, 171, 172–73, 175, 185, 186–87, 189–94, 196–201; French political affairs, 107, 109–13, 125; Italian mainland,

216

Eisenhower, Dwight David
(*cont'd*)
invasion of, 131–39,
142; North Africa (and
TORCH), 104–23, 132;
OVERLORD and fighting
in France, 1–3, 6–9,
104, 137, 140–49, 151,
152–53, 155–65, 171;
Sicily, invasion of, 119,
123, 125, 126, 127, 130,
131; Supreme Com-
mander, Allied Expedi-
tionary Forces, ap-
pointed as, 142
Eisenhower, Earl (brother),
12, 14, 15, 16, 46
Eisenhower, Edgar
(brother), 12, 14–21,
23, 24, 25, 26
Eisenhower, Ida (mother),
13–19, 21, 23, 24–25,
27, 46, 122
Eisenhower, John (son), 57,
60, 75, 76, 77
Eisenhower, Mamie Geneva
Doud (wife), 49, 58, 60,
75, 76, 78, 143
courtship and marriage,
41, 43–44, 45–46, 48
Eisenhower, Milton
(brother), 12, 14, 15,
16, 27, 42, 46, 63, 71
Eisenhower, Roy (brother),
12, 14, 15

France
World War I, 48, 93
World War II, 8, 74, 87,
88, 94, 95, 96, 155–65,
171, 175, 176; Darlan
and Vichy government,
107–08, 110–14, 132;
de Gaulle and Free
French, 108, 111, 112,
113, 125, 149, 160–61;
North Africa (and
TORCH), 88, 95, 102,
104–23, 125, 132; OVER-
LORD, 1–3, 6–9, 104,
133, 137, 139–49, 151–
53; Paris, liberation of,
160–162; ROUNDUP, 96,
104, 105; SLEDGE-
HAMMER, 96, 98, 101,
102, 105
Fredendall, Maj. Gen.
Lloyd, 115–16, 116–17,
117–18

Gault, James, 158
George VI, King of England,
149
Germany
Nazi Party, 89
World War I, 48, 49, 93
World War II, xiv, 2, 3,
6, 9, 74, 77, 87–96, 102,
104–23, 127, 131–35,
137, 138, 141, 142, 144,
146, 147–48, 149, 151,
153, 156–65, 167, 168,

Germany (*cont'd*)
169, 171–73, 175–79,
182–87, 189–94, 196–
201, 203
See also Hitler, Adolf
Giraud, Gen. Henri, 108–13
Grant, Ulysses S., 172
Great Britain
World War I, 49, 93, 102
World War II, xiv, 2, 7,
9, 74, 81, 82, 87, 88, 89,
91–96, 100, 101–02,
104–05, 106–07, 111,
116, 119–23, 126, 127,
132, 133, 135, 136, 137–
38, 141–46, 151, 153,
155–65, 167–69, 171–
73, 175, 181, 185, 186,
187, 189, 190, 191, 192,
194, 196–97, 198, 200,
201, 203, 204
See also Churchill, Winston

Hazlett, Swede, 25–26, 56–57
Hitler, Adolf, 6, 73, 74, 77,
88, 89, 90, 92, 93, 102,
109, 119, 135, 148, 153,
175, 176, 177, 186, 187,
189, 194, 201
Hoover, Herbert, 69, 70

Italy and World War II, 87–
88, 106; invasion of
mainland, 131–39, 142;
invasion of Sicily, 119,
123, 125, 126–27, 130,
131
See also Badoglio, Pietro;
Mussolini, Benito

Japan and World War II, 78,
80, 81, 87, 91, 92, 93,
199

Kasserine Pass, Battle for,
117–19

Leigh-Mallory, Air Marshal
Trafford, 151, 153

MacArthur, Gen. Douglas,
65–74, 97
McAuliffe, Gen. Tony, 182
Marshall, Gen. George, 56,
80–82, 83–84, 86, 87,
91–96, 99, 102, 105,
114, 126, 137, 140, 141,
142–43, 155, 164, 196,
197, 198, 199, 201
Montgomery, Gen. Bernard,
106, 116, 119, 120, 121,
122, 126, 127, 137–38,
145, 151, 153, 155–65,
180, 183–84, 189, 190,
192, 194, 196
and Eisenhower, xiv, 7,
155–59, 162–64, 164–
65, 167–69, 171, 180–
81, 184–85, 203, 206

Mussolini, Benito, 87–88, 131, 132

North Africa, 88, 95, 102, 104–23, 125, 132

OVERLORD, 1–3, 6–9, 104, 133, 137, 139–49, 151–53

Paris, liberation of, 160–62
Patton, Gen. George S., Jr., 51, 52, 77, 106, 118, 119, 122, 126, 127, 130–31, 162, 165, 178, 179, 183, 185, 189, 192
Pershing, Gen. John J., 55, 59, 60
Philippines
    MacArthur and Eisenhower in, 71–75
    World War II, 80, 81, 82, 83, 87

Quezon, Manuel L., 71, 73, 74–75

Ramsay, Adm. Bertram, 8–9
Rommel, Field Marshal Erwin, and Afrika Korps, 88, 102, 106, 116, 117–18, 119
Roosevelt, Franklin D., xiv, 83, 86, 94, 101, 105, 108, 111, 112, 123, 125, 132, 133, 137, 140, 141,

142, 143, 164, 172, 187, 190, 191, 199, 201
ROUNDUP, 96, 104, 105
Russia
    World War I, 48
    World War II, xiv, 2, 88, 89–91, 94, 96, 102, 122, 141, 142, 186, 187, 189, 190, 191, 192, 194, 196, 200, 201
    See also Stalin, Joseph

Sicily, invasion of, 119, 123, 125, 126–27, 130, 131
Simpson, Gen. William, 199, 200
SLEDGEHAMMER, 96, 98, 101, 102, 105
Smith, Gen. Walter Bedell, 7, 99, 140–41, 145, 181–82
Spaatz, Gen. Carl, 136
Stalin, Joseph, xiv, 90, 141–42, 191

Taylor, Gen. Maxwell, 133, 134
Tedder, Air Marshal Arthur, 7, 145, 147, 157, 158
TORCH, 105–06, 108, 109, 110, 113
Truman, Harry, 90

United Nations, 187

West Point (United States Military Academy), 29, 31–32, 34, 35, 40, 66

West Point (*cont'd*)
  Eisenhower at, 26, 27, 31–38, 40
World War I, 48–49, 93, 102
  Eisenhower and, 49–50, 50–51
World War II, xiv, 74, 78, 80, 87
  Ardennes and Battle of the Bulge, 175–79, 182–86
  Berlin, push toward and capture of, xiv, 163, 164, 167, 171–73, 175, 185, 186–87, 189–94, 196–201
  Italian mainland, invasion of, 131–39, 142
  North Africa (and TORCH), 88, 95, 102, 104–23, 125, 132
  OVERLORD and fighting in France, 1–3, 6–9, 104, 133, 137, 139–49, 151–53, 155–65, 171
  ROUNDUP, 96, 104, 105
  Sicily, invasion of, 119, 123, 125, 126–27, 130, 131
  SLEDGEHAMMER, 96, 98, 101, 102, 105

about the author

When Stephen E. Ambrose was Associate Editor of Dwight D. Eisenhower's military papers (published as THE WAR YEARS), he had personal contact with the President himself, as well as access to unpublished material on World War II. His study of Eisenhower's war service, THE SUPREME COMMANDER, followed five earlier books and preceded an important work on American foreign policy, RISE TO GLOBALISM. Born in 1936, Professor Ambrose was Ernest J. King Professor at the Naval War College and Eisenhower Professor of War and Peace at Kansas State University before becoming Professor of History at Louisiana State University in New Orleans.

Format by Anne E. Brown
Set in 12 pt. Bodoni Book
Composed by AMERICAN BOOK–STRATFORD PRESS, INC.
Printed by HALLIDAY LITHOGRAPH CORPORATION
Bound by AMERICAN BOOK–STRATFORD PRESS, INC.
HARPER & ROW, PUBLISHERS, INCORPORATED